A PEOPLE'S GUIDE TO
THE FEDERAL BUDGET

National Priorities Project

written by Mattea Kramer
with Jo Comerford, Samantha Dana, Sheila Heady,
Chris Hellman, Osman Keshawarz, Mia Logg,
Abby Rusk, Becky Sweger, and Ann Werboff

foreword by Barbara Ehrenreich
afterword by Josh Silver

Interlink Books

An imprint of Interlink Publishing Group, Inc.
Northampton, Massachusetts

First published in 2012 by

INTERLINK BOOKS
An imprint of Interlink Publishing Group, Inc.
46 Crosby Street, Northampton, Massachusetts 01060
www.interlinkbooks.com

Library of Congress Cataloging-in-Publication Data

A people's guide to the federal budget / by National Priorities Project.
     p. cm.
ISBN 978-1-56656-887-6 (pbk.)
1. Budget--United States. 2. Government spending policy--United
States. 3. Budget deficits--United States. 4. Fiscal policy--United States.
HJ2051.P476 2012
352.4'973--dc23
                              2012007930

General Editor: Michel S. Moushabeck
Editors: John Fiscella, Leyla Moushabeck
Proofreaders: Gayatri Kumar, Katherine Moonan
Charts and graphs: Daniel Gautreau and National Priorities Project staff
Cover and interior cartoons: Tom Pappalardo
Book design and production: Pam Fontes-May

Printed and bound in the United States of America

10 9 8 7 6 5 4 3 2 1

To request our complete 48-page, full-color catalog, please call us toll
free at 1-800-238-LINK, visit our website at www.interlinkbooks.com,
or send us an e-mail: info@interlinkbooks.com

Dedicated to Greg Speeter,
Founder of National Priorities Project
~an extraordinary visionary~
1943–2012

Table of Contents

Key to A People's Guide to the Federal Budget   x

Federal Spending Categories   xi

Foreword   xiii

1. Why Should You Care about the Federal Budget?   1

2. The Big Picture   5
Speak the Budget Language   5
  • Discretionary and Mandatory Spending   5
  • Budget Authority, Obligations, and Outlays   7
  • Projected and Actual   9
  • Requested and Appropriated   10
  • Gross Domestic Product   10
A Guide to the Numbers   11
  • Inflation   11
  • Per Capita: Scaling by Population   13
  • Fiscal and Calendar Years   14
Now You Speak the Language   14

3. A Brief History of the Federal Budget   19
The Creation of the Treasury Department   20
The Budget and Accounting Act of 1921   21
FDR and WWII   23
Johnson and the Great Society   24
Congressional Budget and Impoundment Control Act of 1974   25

4. Who Decides the Federal Budget?   33
An Evolving Process   33
Before the Budget   34
How Does the Federal Government Create a Budget?   34
  • Step 1: The President Submits a Budget Request   36
  • Step 2: The House and Senate Pass Budget Resolutions   40
  • Step 3: House and Senate Subcommittees "Markup"
    Appropriation Bills   41
  • Step 4: The House and Senate Vote on Appropriations Bills
    and Reconcile Differences   45
  • Step 5: The President Signs Each Appropriations Bill and
    the Budget Becomes Law   46
It's Even Messier than It Sounds   48
  • Political Ideology and Budget Priorities   48
  • Economic Theory and Federal Budget Priorities   50
  • Campaign Money   53
  • Lobbying   54
  • All Politics is Local   56

5. Where Does the Money Come From?   **61**
Income Taxes   63
Corporate Taxes   65
History of Federal Fund Revenues   70
Payroll Taxes   73
Borrowing   75

6. Where Does the Money Go?   **79**
Mandatory and Discretionary Spending   82
Tracking Your Income Tax Dollar   87
  • Are Federal Funds the Same as Discretionary Spending?   87
History of Federal Spending   87

7. The Federal Debt   **103**
Why Do We Borrow?   103
How Does the Federal Government Borrow?   104
History of Federal Deficits   106
History of the Federal Debt   107
Who Lends Money to the Federal Government?   111
Debt Held by the Public   112
Debt Held by Federal Accounts   114
The Debt Ceiling   115
Limiting or Eliminating Federal Deficits   117

8. The President's 2013 Budget Request   **121**
A Couple Bumpy Years for the Federal Budget   121
What *Is* the President's Budget Request?   122
The New Budget   123
  • Discretionary Spending Declines, Mandatory Grows as
    Shares of the Budget   124
  • Where the Money Comes From in 2013   128
  • It's the Economy   128
  • The Deficit   131
  • Health Care Spending Continues to Grow   132
  • Military Spending in 2013 and Beyond   134
  • Funding Education   137

9. Take Action   **141**
Know Who Represents You   142
Register to Vote   142
Stay Informed   143
Contact Your Representatives   143
Phone Calls   143
Writing a Letter or E-mail   145
Social Media   145
Meeting With Your Representative   146
Other Important Ways to Stay Politically Active   147

Afterword   **153**

Appendix: For Educators   **155**
    A Letter to Educators   155
    Two Sample Activators for High School Learners   158
    Two Sample Chapter Activities   159

Appendix: Federal Spending in the States   **163**
    Children's Health Insurance Program   163
    Community Development Block Grant   164
    Head Start   165
    Low Income Energy Assistance Program   167
    Medicaid   168
    National School Lunch Program   169
    Section 8   170
    Temporary Assistance for Needy Families   172
    WIC   173

Appendix: Dashboard for the Proposed 2013 Budget   **175**

About National Priorities Project   **182**

National Priorities Project Team   **184**

Foundation Support   **186**

Glossary of Terms   **187**

List of Figures   **194**

List of Extras   **196**

List of Learn to Fish   **197**

List of Did You Knows   **198**

Endnotes   **199**

Acknowledgements   **219**

Key to *A People's Guide to the Federal Budget*

Throughout *A People's Guide to the Federal Budget*, look for the following symbols to guide you through each chapter:

Glossary additions: When you see words in **bold**, it means you've come across glossary terms. Look for a list of glossary additions at the end of each chapter and a complete glossary at the end of the book.

Did You Know: Check out these quirky facts about the federal budget.

Extra!: Look for these sidebars for more information on topics ranging from earmarks to the Buffett rule.

Learn to Fish: You've heard the old saying, "Give a man a fish, he eats for a day. Teach a man to fish, he eats for life." *A People's Guide to the Federal Budget* teaches you to fish. Look for "Learn to Fish" sidebars that teach you what to look for when you see federal budget numbers, and how to separate substance from spin.

Takeaways: Look for takeaways to summarize key lessons from every chapter.

Federal Spending Categories

In this book, federal spending is divided into the following thirteen categories. These are not official categories designated by the federal government. Rather, they are developed by National Priorities Project and are intended to make the complex federal budget more comprehensible. Here's what's included in each category:

Education: Elementary, secondary, vocational, and higher education.

Energy & Environment: Energy supply, energy use, and natural resource conservation.

Food & Agriculture: Agriculture research, support to agriculture industries, and food assistance programs (including food stamps, WIC, the school lunch program, and others).

Government: Judicial, executive, and legislative branches of government, as well as the postal service.

Housing & Community: Housing assistance, community development, and disaster assistance and relief.

Interest on Debt: The interest payments the federal government makes on its accumulated debt minus interest income received by the government for assets it owns.

International Affairs: Diplomacy, and development and humanitarian activities overseas.

Medicare & Health: Medicare, Medicaid, Children's Health Insurance Program, consumer and occupational health and safety, and other kinds of health services.

Military: The military, war costs, nuclear weapons, and other kinds of security programs.

Science: Scientific research including space programs.

Social Security, Unemployment & Labor: Social Security, Unemployment Insurance, job training, and federal employee retirement and disability programs.

Transportation: Air, water, and ground transportation.

Veterans' Benefits: Health care, housing, education, and income benefits for veterans.

Foreword
by Barbara Ehrenreich

In 1998 I took a job as a waitress at a family restaurant in Key West, Florida, earning $2.43 an hour plus tips. That was the beginning of a journey. I took a series of low-wage jobs so that I could report on the challenges that people across this country face as they try to make ends meet on meager paychecks, and sometimes on no paycheck at all.

One of the prevailing lessons of *Nickel and Dimed* is that the experience of being a working person in America has a lot to do with decisions made in Washington about federal spending. National Priorities Project has responded with *A People's Guide to the Federal Budget* so that the budget isn't some obscure, impenetrable tome but rather something owned and shaped by all of us. Ideally, the federal budget should be an expression of our collective values—including the values of people in middle-income as well as low-income communities, where residents typically have been disenfranchised from most kinds of civic engagement.

The people who appear in *Nickel and Dimed* couldn't always make ends meet on their paychecks, and sometimes they turned to safety-net programs for public assistance. I understand now that differences in federal programs have a pretty profound impact on individual lives. For example anyone who is eligible for the food stamp program and applies for assistance will receive food stamp benefits. As it turns out, that's because funding for that program is part of *mandatory spending* in the federal budget. Mandatory spending isn't a concept most people know much about, but it's in this book. Mandatory spending automatically increases during weak economic times, as more people qualify for benefits from programs like food stamps, and then it shrinks when the economy strengthens and fewer people need public assistance.

I also learned that welfare—the program reformed in the 1990s and renamed Temporary Assistance for Needy Families (TANF)—does not always make assistance available for eligible people who apply for benefits, because TANF is part of what is called *discretionary spending* in the federal budget. That's another concept that isn't common lingo for most people, and one that this book covers in depth. The discretionary budget is determined every year at the discretion of federal lawmakers, and in this age of budget cutting, nonmilitary discretionary spending—which pays for TANF and many other domestic programs—has a bull's-eye on it for deep cuts, even though it comprises only around 12 percent of the total federal budget.

As federal lawmakers cut spending, all 50 states must in turn reduce services they offer to their residents, since federal money helps to fund many programs administered on the state level. It turns out that knowing what discretionary and mandatory spending are, and who decides them, is pretty important to understanding how federal programs reach the people in my own community, and in your community as well. Everyone is affected by the federal budget, whether through income-tax rates, the construction of roads and highways, or funding for law enforcement. We all have a lot at stake when it comes to the way the federal government constructs its budget.

When *Nickel and Dimed* was first published, lots of people asked me what I thought should be done differently in order to help working people. Affordable housing, I said. Health care for all people. Better public schools and better public transportation. That's my wish list, though I realize it may not be *your* wish list.

There's much disagreement about what the role of government should be, and what the federal government can afford. You may well disagree with my priorities. But agree or disagree, you and I both should understand what's in this book. We should understand the many kinds of federal taxes we pay and the ways the government spends that money. We should understand it because it's *our* money making its way through the complicated federal budget process.

And while the federal budget is complicated in any year, in recent years it's gotten much more so. In 2011 there was no federal budget until six months into the fiscal year, and then it was a budget made of something called *continuing resolutions*, which maintained funding for some programs at the same level as the previous year and made across-the-board cuts to other programs. When lawmakers govern with continuing resolutions instead of a real budget, they abdicate their responsibility and make it much harder for voters to understand the budget, let alone hold elected officials accountable for decisions they make on our behalf.

This year the president, the entire House of Representatives, and one-third of the Senate are up for re-election. With more budget cuts in the pipeline, the officials we elect in November will have the opportunity to reshape our country for years to come. If we're to have any hope of navigating the federal budget process and understanding the complex decisions our elected officials will make in future years, we need this book. *A People's Guide to the Federal Budget* is our way in.

Barbara Ehrenreich is a writer and activist from Butte, Montana. She began her education at Reed College in Portland, Oregon, where she received a degree in Physics. She continued on to receive a Ph.D. in Cell Biology at Rockefeller University. Barbara began her career at a small nonprofit that fought for better health care for New York's poor. Since then she has become involved in many issues, working and writing on behalf of them. Currently Barbara works primarily in writing nonfiction books, journal essays, and articles, and activism. To date she has written 21 books and appeared in countless periodicals, primarily reporting on current social issues.

ONE

Why Should You Care about the Federal Budget?

"Democracy is not a spectator sport."
—Barbara Jordan (1936–1996),
The first African American Congresswoman from the Deep South,
and the first woman elected to the Texas Senate

The federal budget affects your hometown, though you may not realize it.

Look around.

If you're used to paved streets and highways, public transportation, streetlights, and police officers who are enforcing laws, then the federal budget plays a role in your hometown and your own life. You might think that these things are funded by your local or state government, and in part that's true. But the trillions of dollars spent by the federal government each year make up a sizable chunk of state budgets, and state governments pass that money down to local cities and towns. Federal money comes right into your own community.

Perhaps you're a college student seeking financial aid. You're likely to apply for a Pell Grant, the federal program that helps students pay for college. Maybe you know a veteran who served in Iraq or Afghanistan and now participates in physical rehabilitation through the Veterans Administration. Or perhaps you get health insurance through your state, or through Medicaid or Medicare. Maybe you are retired and receive a monthly Social Security check, or maybe someone you know relies on unemployment benefits to make ends meet. All of these programs, and countless others, are funded in the federal budget.

Federal programs funnel thousands of dollars to the average American, though few people realize the extent to which government assistance benefits them. One poll asked 1,400 Americans if they had ever used a government program, and 57 percent said no. The same respondents then were asked if they had used any of 21 different programs—everything from unemployment benefits to the home-mortgage interest deduction—and 94 percent said they had used at least one.[1] In other words, there's a lot of confusion about federal spending. Most people don't recognize federal spending even if federal programs provide them with direct assistance.

While many people don't have a clear idea about where federal dollars go, Americans also increasingly believe that the government does not serve their interests. A poll in November 2011 found that people think more than half of every tax dollar is wasted.[2] A March 2011 poll found that Americans are pessimistic about the nation's direction, with nearly two-thirds saying the country is on the wrong track.[3]

Another poll found that 71 percent of respondents wanted to reduce the size of government. But when asked what kinds of spending should be cut, the vast majority strongly opposed cuts to just about every federal program.[4] One of the very few kinds of spending singled out for cuts was international assistance. However, US spending on aid to foreign countries is just 1 percent of the total federal budget.

The federal budget is huge and complicated, and many people find it confusing. That confusion, paired with the growing feeling that the country is on the wrong track, may prevent people from trying to influence the way things are done in Washington. It may prevent them from trying to influence which programs should receive lots of federal dollars and which programs should have their funding cut. It may seem pointless to contact lawmakers or join a protest. Even voting may seem like it doesn't do any good. So if the federal budget is confusing and if people feel like they can't make a difference, then why should you bother?

The US Constitution has the answer: you own the government. The budget may be confusing, but you *can* make a difference, because the federal government answers to you and to all Americans. The United States has a government for the people

Democracy (de·moc·ra·cy)
A government in which the supreme power is vested in the people and exercised by them directly or indirectly through a system of representation usually involving periodically held free elections.[5]

by the people, and that gives all of us both the right and the responsibility to roll up our sleeves and weigh in on the political process.

That may sound daunting. But a little information about the federal budget can go a long way. In February 2011, the nonprofit Center on Policy Attitudes and the University of Maryland joined forces and gave more than a thousand randomly selected people some background information about the budget. Armed with that information, respondents then were asked how they would go about determining priorities for federal spending while reducing budget deficits. Respondents were able to reduce deficits by making choices about spending and tax policies. Majorities of respondents chose to raise taxes on wealthy people and corporations and to reduce military spending.[6]

The late Congresswoman Barbara Jordan said, "Democracy is not a spectator sport." But to get off the sidelines and influence our democracy, you've got to know a little bit about what's going on in Washington. That's likely why, from 1996 to 2002, the White House released its "Citizen's Guide to the Federal Budget" alongside the president's annual budget request.[7] This Citizen's Guide gave key background information to the American people about what the federal government was doing with billions of tax dollars, starting with the basics; the 2002 Citizen's Guide began by asking the question, "What *Is* the Budget?" This guide helped Americans understand the budget as well as how to communicate with elected officials about spending priorities.

Yet 2002 was the last year that the White House put out a Citizen's Guide. *A People's Guide to the Federal Budget* is the new guide for ordinary Americans, to help all people stay informed. Because the more informed you are the more active you're likely to become. And the more active citizens are at the local, state, and national levels—by posting on Facebook, talking with neighbors, contacting elected officials, or joining a protest—the healthier our democracy. In a truly healthy democracy, the government is accountable to all of its people. And when lots of people think the country is on the wrong track, then they speak up and have their voices heard.

Representative Jordan's words were never as true as they were in 2011; democracy is *not* a spectator sport, and our democracy badly needs your participation. Fiscal year 2011 was a bumpy year for the federal budget and for Washington in general, with political gridlock nearly forcing a government shutdown. Indeed, in the last couple of years, the budget process has gone off the rails numerous times and in numerous ways. That's a call to you and to all Americans to watch closely and to speak up about how you believe the federal government should serve its people.

In order to understand when the budget process has gone off the rails, however, first you have to know what it's *supposed* to look like. *A People's Guide to the Federal Budget* is for folks like you across the country so that you can understand the steps of the federal budget process and can identify the impact of federal spending and tax policies on your own family and community. And with a little information, you too can speak up and have your voice heard.

Representative Jordan also said, "If you're going to play the game properly you'd better know every rule."

Let's get started.

TWO

The Big Picture

"In all matters, before beginning,
a diligent preparation should be made."
—Marcus Tullius Cicero, Roman philosopher

The federal budget is complicated. There are lots of steps to creating the annual budget, there are big numbers involved, and it's full of technical jargon. It might sound to you like a foreign language. So before you dive into the big numbers, read this chapter to learn about the language of the federal budget. It begins with some budget terms so you can distinguish between different types of federal spending. Then it links the budget to the economic concept of Gross Domestic Product. Finally, it gives you a guide to the numbers so you know what to look for and what to avoid when you see the numbers of the federal budget.

Speak the Budget Language

One reason the budget may seem so complicated is that you sometimes hear conflicting things about it. You might hear, for instance, that Social Security is the most costly federal program, but then you might hear that the military is the most costly. Both of these statements can't be true, can they?

Discretionary and Mandatory Spending

Well, in a sense both of the above statements *are* true. Perhaps the most important concept in federal budgeting is the difference between mandatory and discretionary spending. **Discretionary spending**, which typically represents around one-third of the total federal budget, is the portion of the budget that the president

requests and Congress **appropriates** every year. An appropriation is a law that authorizes the expenditure of funds for a given purpose. (Chapter 4 covers the president's budget request and the congressional appropriations process in detail.) Discretionary spending has its name because it changes every year at the discretion of lawmakers. Discretionary spending includes funding for programs like education, the environment, and the military. The military is the most expensive discretionary program.

But then there's **mandatory spending**. Mandatory spending refers to money that is spent based on existing laws that govern particular programs. Mandatory spending is *not* part of the annual appropriations process. It includes **entitlement programs**; *entitlement* means that people who are eligible for assistance through such programs must by law receive benefits, hence they are entitled to those benefits. Programs that comprise mandatory spending include Social Security, Medicare, food stamps, and numerous others. Social Security is the most expensive mandatory program. Thus Social Security and the military each is the most expensive federal program of its kind. In 2011 the federal government spent about the same amount of money on each one: $743 billion for all military programs, versus $756 billion on Social Security.[8]

Combined, mandatory and discretionary spending, plus **interest** on federal debt, equal total federal spending. Interest is the fee paid by a borrower to a lender, usually expressed as a percentage of the amount borrowed.

Budget Authority, Obligations, and Outlays

Besides the distinction between mandatory and discretionary spending, another reason you might hear confusing or conflicting things about the federal budget is because there are lots of different ways to measure federal spending. There are different names, and different corresponding numbers, depending on whether you're talking about the federal government's legal authority to spend money, or binding financial contracts to which federal agencies have committed, or actual cash spent by the US Treasury.

When Congress appropriates money for a certain project or program, it provides **budget authority** for spending for that purpose. Budget authority is the legal authority for federal agencies to spend money. This is something that is easy to forget about the US government; federal officials cannot just spend money without first going through a lengthy process to establish the legal authority to do so. Once lawmakers establish budget authority for a particular purpose, federal agencies then can enter into financial **obligations**. Obligations occur when agencies enter into binding agreements—contracts, purchase orders, the hiring of federal workers, and so on—to spend a certain amount of money for a particular good or service. Obligations then result in **outlays**. Outlays are the sums of money actually paid out by the Treasury, primarily by issuing checks or making electronic fund transfers. So depending on which of these three things you're measuring, you might hear different numbers for the size of the federal budget—and the different numbers could all be correct!

It might sound strange that you need to know these three different concepts to talk about the budget, but think of your own personal finances. Perhaps you make a decision to buy a car, and you decide you'll spend no more than $15,000. Then you make an agreement with a car dealership to buy a car for $13,500. Then you pay $200 every month until you've paid off the whole cost of the car. In this case, $15,000 was your budget authority; the agreement to buy the car for $13,500 was your obligation; and the $200 monthly payments are your outlays.

In the federal budget, budget authority is a measure of the budget looking forward; it is lawmakers' expectation about how much money the government will spend for all of its activities, though it may not precisely match up with obligations and outlays. Outlays are the precise measure of how much the federal government actually spent. And obligations are the bridge between the two.

Budget authority and outlays, however, are not equal to each other in any given year. That's because a given year's outlays are the result of both new obligations made in that year *and* obligations from previous years. Return to the car example. The $13,500 for the car is an obligation made in the current year, but you'll be making payments, or outlays, as a result of that obligation for several years to come. Figure 2.1 illustrates the relationship between a year's budget authority and outlays.

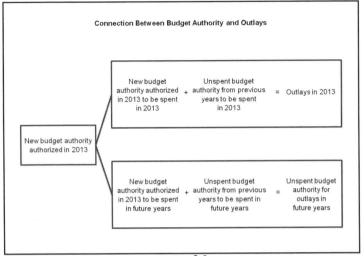

FIGURE 2.1

The relationship between budget authority and outlays varies from program to program and depends on spendout rates. A spendout rate is the rate at which funds appropriated by Congress are obligated and actual payments made. In a program with a high spendout rate, most new budget authority is expended during the fiscal year in which it is approved. For programs with low spendout rates most of the outlays occur in later years.

Projected and Actual

Every February the president issues a budget request, which is officially called the *Budget of the United States Government*. But the numbers in the president's budget are actually just proposed spending; they're only estimates of the amounts that federal agencies will pay out that year. Thus, the numbers in the president's budget request are *proposed* or *projected* spending figures—projections of the spending that will occur if Congress adopts the president's request and if certain assumptions about the economy are accurate. After the end of a fiscal year, the president reports new numbers—*actual* spending.

Generally speaking, when discussing future budgets you're dealing with projected spending, and when looking at past budgets you're seeing actual spending. Chapter 6 of this book is all about how much the federal government spends on different kinds of programs, and all of the numbers for that chapter are for fiscal year 2011. That's because that's the most recent year for which *actual* spending figures are available. This book was published during the 2012 fiscal year, so actual figures for 2012 are not yet known. And in Chapter 8, you'll see the president's *proposed* spending for fiscal year 2013.

Requested and Appropriated

Sometimes you'll hear about requested federal spending and then you'll hear a different number for appropriated funds. The request refers to the amount requested by the president at the start of the annual budget process, while the appropriation refers to the budget authority ultimately granted by Congress. (You'll read a lot more about both of these concepts in Chapter 4.)

Gross Domestic Product

Sometimes federal spending is expressed as a percent of **Gross Domestic Product**. Gross Domestic Product (GDP) is a way of measuring the size of a nation's economy. It's the total value of all final goods and services produced in an economy in a given year. ("Final" means the value of goods and services purchased by the final consumer, as opposed to the value of raw materials purchased by a factory.) GDP is the combined dollar value of all the purchases of final goods by businesses, individuals, and government, plus the value of products exported to foreign countries, minus the value of all of the products imported from other countries. Federal spending is often expressed as a percent of GDP, particularly when comparing the federal budget across different years. That measurement is used because it gives context for the size of the budget by comparing it to the size of the economy as a whole.

So now you can distinguish between mandatory, discretionary, and total spending; requested and appropriated budget authority; obligations and outlays; and the federal budget as a percentage of GDP. Now, on to some numbers.

A Guide to the Numbers

Digging into the federal budget means looking at a lot of numbers. How has the budget's size changed over time? How have revenue sources changed? Which federal programs cost the most? Before looking at the numbers, you've got to make sure you have numbers that are consistent and comparable. You always want to compare apples to apples and not apples to oranges, as the old saying goes.

Inflation

One important thing to consider when comparing numbers from different years is the effect of inflation. **Inflation** is an increase in the average price level in an economy. One typical measure of inflation is the Consumer Price Index (CPI), which is a measure of change in the price of a broad sample of consumer goods. The federal government uses the CPI as one important measure of inflation. In the US economy, inflation is usually around two or three percent a year. That suggests that a can of soda that costs $1 this year will cost $1.02 or $1.03 next year. In practice, though, a can of soda may stay the same price for several years, and then it may make a big jump in price, for example from $1 to $1.10.

The Secret Service Was Created to Prevent Inflation

During the US Civil War, when the Union government first printed paper money, counterfeiting was rampant. The abundance of fake bills in the money supply made the dollar less valuable. On April 14, 1865, President Lincoln created the Secret Service to track down and punish counterfeiters. Later the same day, President Lincoln was shot. Years later, the Secret Service became what it is today, guards who keep the president safe.[9]

A **nominal** dollar amount is one that is not adjusted for inflation; it is the cost or value of something expressed as its price in the year it was purchased. For example, if in 2006 you paid $9 for a movie ticket, then the ticket's nominal price is $9.

A **real** number is a number that has been adjusted for inflation. Adjusting for inflation requires converting nominal dollar figures into dollars from a single year, which is called the base year. This conversion is calculated using a deflator, a number that changes the value of dollars from one year into another year based on the overall difference in prices between those two years. One such deflator is the CPI. A second common deflator, and the one used in this book, is the GDP deflator. The GDP deflator is a measure of the price level of goods and services produced in this country in a given year, whereas the CPI measures the prices of only some consumer goods.

Back to the movie ticket example. If you convert the $9 ticket price in 2006 into current dollars, you'd have the *real* ticket price—roughly $10 instead of $9. If the total money people spent on movie tickets in 2006 was $9.5 billion and the total amount in 2012 was $10 billion, are more people going to the movies? Or is this increase due to the fact that ticket prices have increased because of inflation? First you have to adjust the numbers for inflation, and then you can answer that question.

Why are these distinctions important for *A People's Guide to the Federal Budget*? If federal spending increases by $250 billion dollars over five years, for example, it is important to know whether that is a *real* increase in the size of the budget. Otherwise, the increase is just the result of inflation.

Let's look at an example using federal outlays in 2000 and 2009. In the following table are nominal and real outlays; the real outlays are expressed in 2013 dollars. Notice that the nominal figures suggest that outlays nearly doubled between 2000 and 2009. But in real terms, outlays increased by 58.3 percent, not by 96.6 percent. So, much of the increase in federal spending over those years is just the effect of inflation. That's why it's always important to know whether you're looking at real or nominal figures. If you're comparing numbers from year to year, it's essential that the numbers are expressed in inflation-adjusted terms.

	2000	2009	Percent Change from 2000 to 2009
Nominal Outlays (in millions of nominal dollars)	$1,788,950	$3,517,677	96.6 percent
Real Outlays (in millions of 2013 dollars)	$2,338,863	$3,701,931	58.3 percent

FIGURE 2.2 NOMINAL OUTLAYS AND REAL OUTLAYS

This book converts just about everything into 2013 dollars so it's easy to compare numbers from year to year. Since this book was published in 2012, converting to 2013 dollars relies on projections of inflation for next year.

Per Capita: Scaling by Population

Another important concept when comparing numbers is **per capita**. Per capita means "per person," and it means that a number—for instance GDP or total federal spending—has been divided by population to show the number on a per-person basis. A sizeable portion of the federal budget is allocated to state governments, and that makes the concept of per capita extremely important. For example, large states tend to receive more federal money than small states. However, if you compare per capita federal spending, large states do not necessarily receive more money.

For example, in fiscal 2010 the federal government granted California $1.63 billion for the Children's Health Insurance Program (CHIP), while it granted New Hampshire $15.54 million.[10] That suggests that California received over one hundred times the federal CHIP money that New Hampshire did. But California is a much larger state, so these numbers would be more useful in per capita terms. Since CHIP is a program for children, it makes sense to divide CHIP funding by each state's child population, rather than total population, to see CHIP dollars per child. Or you can even divide CHIP money by the number of CHIP enrollees in each state instead of the total child population, so that you can see dollars per participant. Figure 2.3 does both.

State	Total FY 2010 federal CHIP funding	Dollars per child	Dollars per participant
California	$1.63 billion	$175	$941
New Hampshire	$15.54 million	$55	$1,462

FIGURE 2.3 CHIP SPENDING PER CHILD AND PER PARTICIPANT

This suggests a very different picture than simply saying that California received one hundred times more federal CHIP funding than New Hampshire. In per-child terms, California received more than three times as much federal funding as New Hampshire did. But in per-participant terms, New Hampshire received more federal money.

Fiscal and Calendar Years

The difference between the fiscal and calendar year is another important consideration when looking at federal budget numbers. The federal budget does not operate on a calendar year, which runs from January 1 to December 31. Instead, the budget is on a **fiscal year**. The federal fiscal year runs from October 1 through September 30. In other words, fiscal year 2013 runs from October 1, 2012, through September 30, 2013. When comparing numbers from different sources, all numbers should be for fiscal years, or all numbers should be for calendar years, but you shouldn't mix and match. For example, taxes are calculated based on a calendar year. Total tax revenues in the 2011 calendar year, however, are not the same as total tax revenues in the 2011 fiscal year because those two years span different months.

Now You Speak the Language

In Chapter 1 you read that many Americans feel confused about the federal budget, and how that confusion likely keeps people from speaking up about their own priorities for where their federal tax dollars should go. Now that you know many of the key concepts in the language of the federal budget, you're well on your way to overcoming any such confusion. In fact, you're on your way to becoming a budget expert. The next chapters of *A People's Guide* have everything you need. Chapter 3 gives you the history of the budget and describes how the federal budget process is still evolving today, as the concerns and priorities of lawmakers and the American public change with time. Chapter 4 provides all the detail you need about how Congress and the president together create the annual budget and how other forces—like politics and economics—also shape the budget process.

Then *A People's Guide* takes you into the numbers. Chapter 5 tells you how the federal government raises the trillions of dollars it spends each year, and Chapter 6 tells you where the federal government spends those trillions of dollars. Chapter 7 explains the concepts of budget deficits and the federal debt, and then Chapter 8 brings you right up to today, with detail about President Obama's budget request for the 2013 fiscal year. Finally, Chapter 9 returns to the notion of democracy. Americans have a right and a responsibility to weigh in on the political process, and Chapter 9 gives you effective tools and tips to do just that.

1) Discretionary spending is the federal spending that the president requests and Congress appropriates every year. Mandatory spending is federal spending determined by existing laws governing certain programs, and does not go through the appropriations process.

2) Budget authority, obligations, and outlays are all different measures of the federal budget. Budget authority is the federal government's legal authority to spend money; obligations occur when the federal government enters into contracts to spend a certain amount of money; and outlays occur when the US Treasury actually spends the money.

3) There are lots of things to consider when looking at the numbers of the federal budget:
   - When comparing numbers from different years, make sure they are adjusted for inflation.
   - Some numbers, like federal money granted to the

states, are most useful when they're expressed in per capita terms.

- The federal fiscal year differs from the calendar year, so you shouldn't mix and match federal budget numbers expressed in fiscal years with numbers expressed in calendar years.

Appropriation is a law that authorizes the expenditure of funds for a given purpose.

Budget Authority is the federal government's legal authority to spend a given amount of money for a certain purpose, according to laws passed by Congress and the president.

Discretionary Spending is the portion of the budget that the president requests and Congress appropriates every year. It represents roughly one-third of the total annual federal budget.

Entitlement Programs are a certain kind of federal program in which all people who are eligible for the program's benefits, according to eligibility rules written into law, must by law receive those benefits if they apply for them. The Supplemental Nutrition Assistance Program, commonly known as food stamps, is an example of an entitlement program; anyone who qualifies and applies for benefits receives food stamps.

Fiscal Year for the federal budget runs from October 1 through September 30. Thus, fiscal year 2013 runs from October 1, 2012, through September 30, 2013.

Gross Domestic Product (GDP) is a way of measuring the size of a nation's economy. It's the total value of all final goods and services produced in an economy in a given year. "Final" means the value of goods and services purchased by the final consumer, as opposed to the value of raw materials purchased by a factory.

Inflation is an increase in the average price level in an economy.

Interest is the fee paid by a borrower to a lender, usually expressed as a percentage of the amount borrowed.

Mandatory Spending is federal money that is spent based on existing laws that govern particular programs, such as entitlement programs like Social Security or food stamps. Mandatory spending is *not* part of the annual appropriations process.

Nominal dollar amounts are not adjusted for inflation; they are the cost or value of something expressed as its price in the year it was purchased. For example, if in 2006 you paid $9 for a movie ticket, then the ticket's nominal price is $9.

Obligations are binding financial agreements entered into by the federal government. Examples of obligations include contracts, purchase orders, and the hiring of federal workers

Outlays are money paid out by the US Treasury; they occur when obligations are actually paid off, primarily by issuing checks or making electronic fund transfers.

Per Capita means "per person." For example, per capita GDP is GDP divided by population, which shows GDP on a per-person basis.

Real numbers have been adjusted for inflation.

THREE

A Brief History of the Federal Budget

"E pluribus unum"
"Out of many, one"
—Phrase on the Seal of the United States

The US Constitution doesn't specify a process for creating a federal budget. The process that's used today was developed over centuries, and it's still changing. That makes it all the more important for you and all Americans to understand the process and to speak up when it doesn't serve your needs. Your voice—and your vote—has the potential to change the way the federal budget is created each year.

From the beginning of US history through the twentieth century and today, the needs and values of the nation and the concerns of the president and Congress have influenced the budget process and shaped the role and size of the federal government. As the priorities of lawmakers and the American public change over time, so too does the federal budget; new programs are established while outdated ones are discontinued.

During the Great Depression, the driving force behind changes to the budgetary process and the role of federal agencies were the will of the people and the aspirations of government officials to put people back to work and assist them during hard times. Later, during the 1960s, concerns for the poor and underserved populations compelled the creation of new government programs like Medicare and Medicaid. Currently, concerns over the weak economy as well as size of the budget are shaping discussions about the role of the government.

The Creation of the Treasury Department

The First Congress of the United States convened in New York City on March 4, 1789, marking the beginning of the US government under the newly ratified Constitution. Congress enacted legislation creating the Department of the Treasury in September of that year to serve as a permanent institution to manage the government's finances.[11]

Yet the functioning of a national treasury had actually begun almost fourteen years earlier, as the First Continental Congress in Philadelphia struggled to pay for the War of Independence against Great Britain. The Congress had no power to levy and collect taxes. With no income and no actual sovereignty, it also had no way to attract loans from foreign governments or international investors. No one was willing to lend money to an entity that was not officially recognized outside of its own, self-proclaimed area of jurisdiction and had no reliable source of revenue with which to repay its debts. To raise funds the delegates to the Second Continental Congress decided to issue paper money in the form of bills of credit. These were essentially IOUs issued on faith in the revolution to be redeemed at a later date.[12] The Congress later instructed the colonies to contribute to the treasury, yet the lack of formal political and economic ties between the colonies and Congress resulted in little financial support.

The Hamilton-Burr Duel

Alexander Hamilton, the first Treasury Secretary, was General George Washington's aide-de-camp during the Revolutionary War.[13] He was killed by sitting Vice President Aaron Burr in 1804 in a pistol duel that arose from long-standing political and personal bitterness between the two.[14]

The revolution's financial situation changed dramatically during the Second Continental Congress with the signing of the Declaration of Independence. Thereafter the new republic was

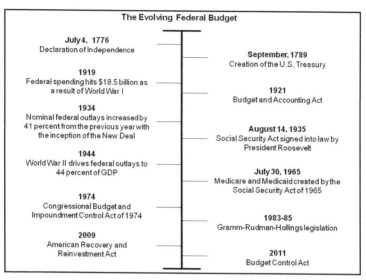

FIGURE 3.1

able to attract loans overseas and at home. Yet despite the influx of resources, creation of an institution capable of managing a unified national budget remained a challenge. The Treasury Office itself was reorganized three times between 1778 and 1781.[15]

The Budget and Accounting Act of 1921

The first major piece of legislation regarding the budget process was the Budget and Accounting Act of 1921,[16] which was enacted to improve federal financial management after World War I. Wartime spending between 1916 and 1919 had increased the nominal national debt by over $23 billion[17] and members of Congress felt they needed greater control over federal spending.

The main impact of the 1921 Budget Act was on the executive branch. In fact, it established many of the key agencies involved in today's development and oversight of the federal budget. It did not, however, directly alter congressional procedures for making revenue and spending decisions.

The Act created the Bureau of the Budget, which was later renamed the Office of Management and Budget (OMB), which reports to the office of the president. OMB gives guidelines to federal agencies for the preparation of strategic plans and budgets.

It also serves as the president's accounting office. Furthermore, the 1921 Act required the administration to submit an annual budget to Congress. In addition, the Act created the General Accounting Office—which was later renamed the Government Accountability Office (GAO)—to audit federal spending.[18] The GAO still exists today; see the end of this chapter for more about it.

The Statistical Abstract of the United States

The Statistical Abstract is "the authoritative and comprehensive summary of statistics on the social, political, and economic organization of the United States."[19] It has been published since 1878, when it catalogued the value of the wheat and tobacco harvests in the US that year.[20] Figure 3.2 shows what the old Statistical Abstract looked like.

No. 149.—ESTIMATED PRODUCTION, AREA, and VALUE of the TOBACCO CROP of the UNITED STATES, from 1868 to 1877, inclusive.a

YEAR.	Product.	Area.	Values.	Value per pound.	Yield per acre.	Value per acre.
	Pounds.	Acres.	Dollars.	Cents.	Pounds.	Dollars.
1868	402,000,000	536,000	42,612,000	10.6	750	79 50
1869	393,000,000	604,000	41,205,000	10.5	651	68 32
1870	385,000,000	575,000	38,500,000	10	669	66 90
1871	426,000,000	580,000	41,748,000	9.8	734	71 96
1872	480,000,000	584,600	49,920,000	10.4	821	85 39
1873	506,000,000	653,000	41,998,000	8.3	775	64 32
1874	315,000,000	500,000	34,650,000	11	630	69 30
1875	522,000,000	710,000	41,760,000	8	735	58 81
1876	535,000,000	733,000	39,590,000	7.4	730	54 01
1877	580,000,000	745,000	40,600,000	7	778	54 49

FIGURE 3.2 THE STATISTICAL ABSTRACT

In more recent times, the Statistical Abstract has catalogued the trillions of dollars spent by the federal government each year. However, the US Census Bureau terminated the collection of data for the Statistical Abstract, effective October 1, 2011, due to budget cuts.[21]

Prior to enactment of the 1921 Budget Act, the federal government had no formal process for developing and producing a budget. Congress created and amended its own rules regarding the appropriation of funds, leaving little opportunity for input by the president. By requiring the president to submit an annual budget proposal, the Act shifted a significant amount of control over the federal budget to the executive branch. Congress was expected to fulfill its revenue and spending functions if it was given comprehensive budget recommendations by the president.

Yet in the 1920s federal spending remained low. The federal budget did not play the same role in the larger economy that it does today, in which government spending is over 20 percent of the Gross Domestic Product (GDP).[22] Instead, the government played a role in developing the economy through policy decisions. For example, the government gave public land to railroad companies in order to speed the "opening of the west" and set low mining fees on public lands to encourage mining.

A Second Bill of Rights

Referred to as the Economic Bill of Rights, President Roosevelt asserted that all Americans have the right to a job and an adequate wage; the right to a home, medical care, and education; and the right to protection from economic hardship that results from illness, accident, age, or unemployment.[23]

FDR and WWII

The role of the government changed dramatically during the 1930s. When Franklin D. Roosevelt began his first term as president in March 1933, he was confronted by a nation mired in the depths of the Great Depression. In his inaugural speech, President Roosevelt said, "This nation asks for action, and action now. Our greatest primary task is to put people to work."[24] In his first 100 days in office, President Roosevelt worked with a special session of

Congress to enact a series of laws that, along with a number of presidential executive orders,[25] provided a framework for what became known as "the New Deal."

New Deal programs covered a range of issues, including the historic creation of the **Social Security** system to provide income for retirees. Social Security, officially called the Old Age, Survivors, and Disability Insurance program, is a federal program that is meant to ensure that elderly and disabled people do not live in poverty. There were also numerous programs intended to create jobs, such as the Civilian Conservation Corps, the Civil Works Administration, and the Tennessee Valley Authority. To create these jobs, the government pumped billions of dollars into the US economy. Nominal federal outlays grew from $4.6 billion in 1933 to $6.5 billion in 1934, an increase of 41 percent in one year.[26] (Only nominal figures are available for these historical numbers.) The budget continued to grow, albeit more slowly, until the US entry into World War II in 1941, after which it rose significantly. At the height of the war in 1944, outlays reached an all-time high of 44 percent of GDP.[27]

Johnson and the Great Society

The next major change to the federal budget did not occur until the 1960s. President Lyndon Johnson, in his 1964 State of the

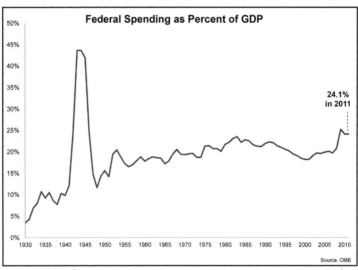

FIGURE 3.3 (THIS CHART ALSO APPEARS IN CHAPTER 6 AS FIGURE 6.8)

Union address, called for a "war on poverty" in America.[28] During his presidency, programs including Medicare, Medicaid, Head Start, the Elementary and Secondary Education Act, and the Jobs Corps were all enacted as part of President Johnson's "Great Society," dramatically expanding the role of government, and with it, the size of the federal budget.

As Figure 3.4 shows, the Great Society in the 1960s corresponded with growth in the size of the federal budget, with a gradually increasing percentage of the budget taken up by mandatory spending on Social Security and need-based programs like Medicaid and food stamps.

Congressional Budget and Impoundment Control Act of 1974

The framework for the current budget process was established in the Congressional Budget and Impoundment Control Act of 1974. Congress passed the 1974 Act because lawmakers were concerned that the congressional budget process was too disorganized. Many

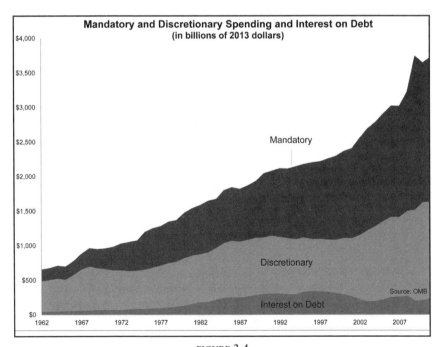

FIGURE 3.4

25

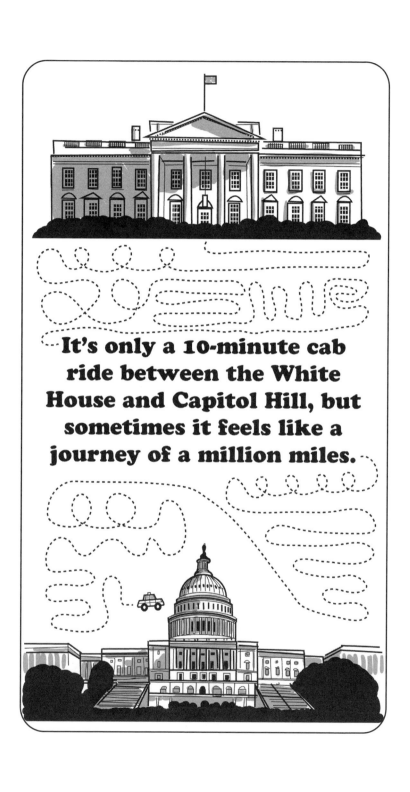

It's only a 10-minute cab ride between the White House and Capitol Hill, but sometimes it feels like a journey of a million miles.

also felt that the president exercised too much control over federal budgeting.[29] During the Nixon administration in particular, members of Congress worried about the president's ability to block the spending of funds that already had been authorized and appropriated by Congress.[30]

The 1974 Act strengthened Congress's role in the budget process. It created the House and Senate Budget Committees to co-ordinate congressional action on the budget and the Congressional Budget Office (CBO) to provide nonpartisan analysis and information on the budget and the economy. (Read more about the CBO at the end of this chapter.) The legislation required an annual budget resolution both in the House and Senate, which gives Congress the opportunity to determine its budget priorities for the coming year and specify overall levels for spending and taxation.

Over the five decades since World War II, federal spending as a percentage of GDP peaked in 1983 during the Reagan military build-up and then again in 2009 in response to the Great Recession. During the 1990s, federal spending fell as a percentage of GDP, as the economy grew briskly but federal spending increased at a slower rate.[31] By the end of that decade, federal spending was at a low not seen for almost 35 years.

More recently, federal spending has grown significantly due to increases in military spending, rising health care costs, and increased numbers of people retiring and collecting Social Security benefits. Federal spending peaked in 2009 after the Great Recession due to a greater demand for safety-net programs such as unemployment benefits and with the enactment of the 2009 American Recovery and Reinvestment Act.

In recent decades, Congress has passed new laws regulating the budget process—including the Gramm-Rudman-Hollings legislation[32] of the 1980s, which created a mechanism for controlling the annual deficit through a process of automatic spending cuts, and the recently enacted Budget Control Act of 2011.[33] That legislation created a process to reduce the federal debt by $2.4 trillion over ten years. However, the 1974 Budget Control Act remains the basic framework for the current annual budget process. (For more about the Budget Control Act of 2011 and other recent developments in the budget process, see Chapter 8.)

1) Over the course of our nation's history, the size of the federal budget has fluctuated as the result of shifting policy decisions made by the government to take on new roles and responsibilities.
2) For nearly four decades, the Congressional Budget and Impoundment Control Act of 1974 has served as the basic framework for federal budgeting.
3) The current budget process has evolved over time, and it continues to do so.

Social Security, officially called the Old Age, Survivors, and Disability Insurance program, is a federal program that is meant to ensure that elderly and disabled people do not live in poverty. It is funded through payroll taxes.

Key Government Agencies Involved in the Federal Budget

THE OFFICE OF MANAGEMENT AND BUDGET (OMB)

Web site: http://www.omb.gov

What it is: The Office of Management and Budget (OMB) was created under the Budget and Accounting Act of 1921. OMB oversees development and execution of the annual budgets of federal agencies like the Environmental Protection Agency and the Food and Drug Administration. It also oversees agency performance, coordinates and reviews federal regulations developed by the agencies, clears all legislative communications with Congress, and ensures agency compliance with, and implementation of, executive orders and presidential memoranda.

Who's in charge: The Director of OMB is appointed by the president and confirmed by the US Senate, and serves at the president's discretion for an unspecified term. The current acting director is Jeffrey Zients, who took the job in early 2012 when previous director Jacob J. Lew left the position to become President Obama's chief of staff.

What it has for you: The OMB is the single most important resource for materials and analyses related to the president's annual budget request. It also provides budget-related information related to past and proposed federal initiatives.

GOVERNMENT ACCOUNTABILITY OFFICE (GAO)

Web site: http://www.gao.gov

What it is: The Government Accountability Office (GAO) was created by the Budget and Accounting Act of 1921. GAO is Congress's independent, nonpartisan auditing agency. GAO investigates how the federal government spends taxpayer dollars.

GAO's work is done at the request of congressional committees or subcommittees or is mandated by public laws or committee reports. GAO also does independent research under the authority of the Comptroller General (see below). GAO's oversight function includes auditing federal agencies to ensure that funds are being spent properly, investigating allegations of illegal or improper agency actions, reporting on whether government programs or policies are meeting their objectives, analyzing and outlining policy options for Congress, and issuing legal opinions or decisions on agency actions and rules.

Who's in charge: The head of GAO, the Comptroller General of the United States, is appointed to a 15-year term by the president from a slate of candidates proposed by Congress. The current comptroller general is Gene L. Dodaro. He was confirmed by the Senate in 2010.

What it has for you: As a watchdog organization, the GAO provides valuable analysis about cost overruns in federal programs and their causes, projections about how to achieve greater program efficiencies, and whether federal agencies are in compliance with federal statutes or congressional directives.

CONGRESSIONAL BUDGET OFFICE (CBO)

Web site: http://www.cbo.gov

What it is: The Congressional Budget Office (CBO) was created in 1974 under the Congressional Budget and Impoundment Control Act. The CBO supports the budget-related work of Congress by providing objective and nonpartisan analysis to inform the economic and budgetary decisions related to the federal budget. In accordance with its mandate to provide objective and impartial analysis, CBO's reports do not contain policy recommendations.

CBO's work includes short-term and long-term analysis of the federal budget and the broader outlook for the economy, analysis of the president's budget request, and analysis of the spending and revenue effects of legislation. The CBO also regularly publishes a set of budget options that present a wide range of proposals that address changes in spending and taxes.

Who's in charge: The CBO director is appointed jointly by leaders of the House and Senate after considering recommendations made by the two budget committees. The term of office is four years, with no limit on the number of terms a director may serve. Douglas W. Elmendorf is the current CBO director. He has been in the position since 2009.

What it has for you: The CBO is a great resource for information on the long-term effects of federal spending decisions, the costs of federal programs, and the projected costs or revenues of specific program changes or legislative proposals.

CONGRESSIONAL RESEARCH SERVICE (CRS)
Web site: http://www.loc.gov/crsinfo/
What it is: The Congressional Research Service (CRS) was created by Congress in 1914. CRS works exclusively for Congress, providing policy and legal analysis to committees and members of both the House and Senate, regardless of party affiliation. While CRS does not have an explicit role in the budget process, it provides a wealth of analysis that helps lawmakers determine budget priorities.

Who's in charge: The director of CRS is appointed by the Librarian of Congress in consultation with the Joint Committee on the Library. The current director is Mary Mazanec. She was appointed in December 2011.

What it has for you: As Congress's research arm, CRS is a valued and respected source of information and non-partisan analysis on every issue that comes before Congress. Unfortunately CRS materials are not made directly available to the general public. They can, however, be found republished on numerous sites on the Internet, or you can request materials through the offices of members of Congress.

FOUR

Who Decides the Federal Budget?

"Laws are like sausages.
It is better not to see them being made."
—Otto von Bismarck,
German general and politician (1815–1898)

The vision of democracy is that the federal budget—and all activities of the federal government—reflects the values of a majority of Americans. Yet most people feel that the federal budget does not currently reflect their values and that the budgeting process is too complex to understand, as indicated by the public opinion polls described in Chapter 1.

It is indeed a complicated process. A host of forces shapes the federal budget, and some of them are forces written into law—like the president's role in drafting the budget—while some of them are de facto forces that stem from the realities of our political system. This chapter describes it all, from congressional Appropriations Committees to the treadmill of campaign fundraising.

And while a majority of Americans may feel the federal budget does not currently reflect their values, the ultimate power over the US government lies with the people, because we have a right and responsibility to choose our elected officials by voting. Many Americans feel that it is difficult or impossible to make their voices heard in Washington, but the first step is to understand what's going on.

An Evolving Process

The Constitution designates the "power of the purse" as a function of Congress.[34] It includes the authority to create and collect taxes and to borrow money as needed. However, the Constitution does not specify how Congress should go about exercising these powers; it says nothing about how the budgeting process should take place. Nor does the Constitution specify a role for the president in managing the nation's finances.

Since the Constitution does not mandate a budget process, lawmakers have established a process over time. Over the course of the twentieth century, Congress passed key laws that shaped the budgeting process into what it is today, and formed the federal agencies that provide oversight and research crucial to creating the budget.[35] Chapter 3 describes the evolution of these laws in detail.

Before the Budget

The annual budget process in Congress officially is called the **appropriations process**. **Appropriations bills** specify how much money will go to different agencies and programs. But before Congress can appropriate money for everything from building roads to buying milk for elementary school students, Congress first must pass laws stating that the federal government is in the business of building roads and buying milk.[36] Those laws are called **authorizations**. Authorizations often cover multiple years, so authorizing legislation does not need to pass Congress every year the way appropriations bills do. When a multiyear authorization expires, Congress often passes new legislation to continue the programs in question—that's called reauthorization.[37]

Authorizations also serve another purpose. There are some types of spending that are not subject to the appropriations process. Such spending is called direct or mandatory spending, and Chapter 6 explains this in detail. Authorizations provide the legal authority for mandatory spending.[38]

How Does the Federal Government Create a Budget?

There are five key steps in the federal budget process:
Step 1: The president submits a budget request
Step 2: The House and Senate pass budget resolutions
Step 3: House and Senate subcommittees "markup" appropriations bills

Step 4: The House and Senate vote on appropriations bills and reconcile differences

Step 5: The president signs each appropriations bill and the budget becomes law

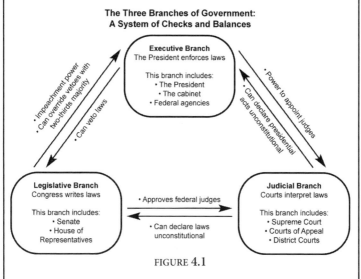

The Three Branches of Government

The structure of the US government is set out in the Constitution and is based on the doctrine of a separation of power. The Constitution calls for three branches of government—legislative, executive, and judicial—to ensure that no individual or small group of individuals has too much control. Power is spread out, with each of the three branches restrained by the others through a system known as checks and balances.

The Three Branches of Government:
A System of Checks and Balances

Executive Branch
The President enforces laws

This branch includes:
• The President
• The cabinet
• Federal agencies

• Impeachment power
• Can override vetoes with two-thirds majority
• Can veto laws

• Power to appoint judges
• Can declare presidential acts unconstitutional

Legislative Branch
Congress writes laws

This branch includes:
• Senate
• House of Representatives

• Approves federal judges

• Can declare laws unconstitutional

Judicial Branch
Courts interpret laws

This branch includes:
• Supreme Court
• Courts of Appeal
• District Courts

FIGURE 4.1

The legislative branch consists of Congress—the House of Representatives and Senate—whose primary functions include the enactment of laws and creating the government's annual budget. The executive branch is made up of the office of the president and the federal agencies.

The main functions of the executive branch are the implementation and enforcement of federal laws and oversight of federal programs. The judicial branch consists of the Supreme Court, the Courts of Appeal, and the District Courts, and their role is to interpret federal laws and determine if they comply with the laws of the Constitution.

Not only does the Constitution grant each branch certain powers, it grants each branch certain powers *over the others*—the checks and balances. For example, Congress enacts laws, but the president can veto them. Congress can override the president's veto, but the Supreme Court can strike down any law it finds unconstitutional. Supreme Court justices serve for life, but they are appointed by the president and confirmed by the Senate, and they can be impeached. Congress must approve the budgets of the executive and the judicial branches, but Congress also has its own budget, which the president can veto. This interlocking system is intended to prevent each branch of government from gaining too much power.[39]

Step 1: The President Submits a Budget Request

The president sends a **budget request** to Congress each February for the coming fiscal year, which will begin on October 1.[40] For example, President Obama submitted his budget request for fiscal year 2013 in February of 2012. Fiscal year 2013 commences on October 1, 2012, and ends on September 30, 2013.

The president's budget request is just a proposal. Congress then reviews the request and passes its own appropriations bills; only after the president signs these bills does the country have a budget for the new fiscal year.[41] Though it is only a proposal, the president's request is officially referred to as the *Budget of the United States Government*.[42] The president's budget contains projections of spending, revenue, borrowing, and debt. It may also contain policy and legislative recommendations guiding the activities of federal agencies and the creation of new (or the termination of old) federal programs.[43] It gives detailed estimates of the financial operations of federal agencies and programs, and data on past and projected circumstances in the economy, like unemployment and inflation. The budget also contains justifications to support the president's recommendations.

To begin the process of writing the president's budget request, the president and Cabinet members decide policy priorities for each federal agency. Based on these priorities, the Office of Management and Budget (OMB), which is part of the executive branch and serves as the White House accounting office, gives instructions to each federal agency—such as the United States Department of Agriculture and the Environmental Protection Agency—on how to construct its budget for the coming year.[44] Each agency then submits its own budget request to OMB and writes documents defending the request, called budget justifications. OMB evaluates these documents and draws on them to prepare the president's budget request, which the president then releases to the public.

The president's budget request follows a lengthy preparation process. Even as a new fiscal year begins, work is already underway at OMB to craft the next year's budget. In other words, work on the fiscal year 2013 request began in the spring of 2011, before fiscal year 2012 had started.[45] And while the process of creating the budget request generally occurs outside the public eye—like the part of an iceberg that's underwater—it is not a closed process. Administration officials get input from members of Congress and staff, particularly on policy issues, in an effort to pave the way for easy adoption of the president's request in Congress. Agency officials may also work with interest groups as they develop their budgets. For example, the Environmental Protection Agency may seek input from environmental advocacy organizations; by doing so, that agency would garner additional support for its budget request, and that would help the budget pass Congress. And even when administration or agency leaders do not seek outside input, lobbyists constantly try to influence federal officials and the purse strings they control. (You'll see more about lobbyists later in this chapter.)

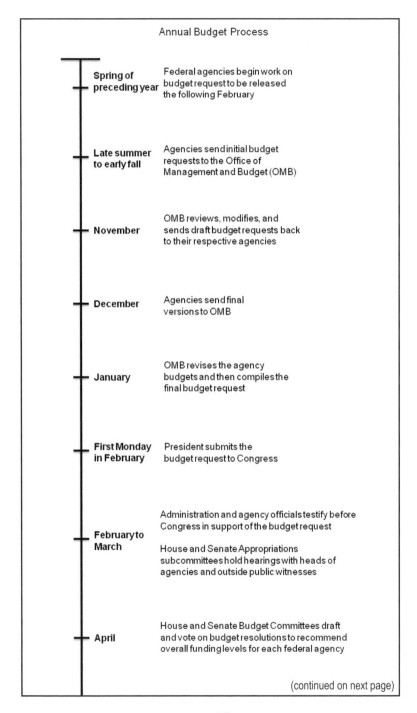

Annual Budget Process

Spring of preceding year — Federal agencies begin work on budget request to be released the following February

Late summer to early fall — Agencies send initial budget requests to the Office of Management and Budget (OMB)

November — OMB reviews, modifies, and sends draft budget requests back to their respective agencies

December — Agencies send final versions to OMB

January — OMB revises the agency budgets and then compiles the final budget request

First Monday in February — President submits the budget request to Congress

February to March — Administration and agency officials testify before Congress in support of the budget request

House and Senate Appropriations subcommittees hold hearings with heads of agencies and outside public witnesses

April — House and Senate Budget Committees draft and vote on budget resolutions to recommend overall funding levels for each federal agency

(continued on next page)

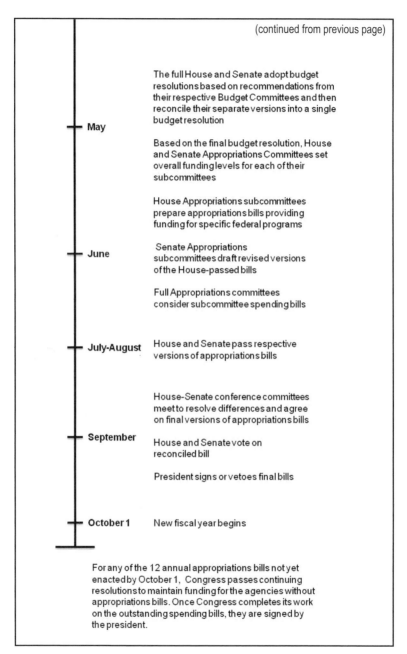

(continued from previous page)

May

The full House and Senate adopt budget resolutions based on recommendations from their respective Budget Committees and then reconcile their separate versions into a single budget resolution

Based on the final budget resolution, House and Senate Appropriations Committees set overall funding levels for each of their subcommittees

House Appropriations subcommittees prepare appropriations bills providing funding for specific federal programs

June

Senate Appropriations subcommittees draft revised versions of the House-passed bills

Full Appropriations committees consider subcommittee spending bills

July-August

House and Senate pass respective versions of appropriations bills

House-Senate conference committees meet to resolve differences and agree on final versions of appropriations bills

September

House and Senate vote on reconciled bill

President signs or vetoes final bills

October 1

New fiscal year begins

For any of the 12 annual appropriations bills not yet enacted by October 1, Congress passes continuing resolutions to maintain funding for the agencies without appropriations bills. Once Congress completes its work on the outstanding spending bills, they are signed by the president.

FIGURE 4.2

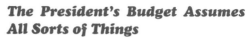

The President's Budget Assumes All Sorts of Things

To project how much tax revenue the government will collect and to estimate how much it will spend on things like unemployment benefits, the president's budget request has to make many assumptions about what will happen in the economy in the coming year.[46]

But those assumptions can be wrong. If the budget request assumes that the economy will be stronger than it ultimately is, then tax revenues likely will be less than expected and spending likely will be higher, as more people qualify for need-based help. Then the government will run a bigger deficit than the budget predicted. (See Chapter 7 for more on deficits.)

Despite this long and involved process, Congress is under no obligation to adopt the president's recommendations.[47] Still, the president's power to formulate the request—which officially is referred to as the US budget—allows the White House to set out its vision for the country.[48] This vision then influences revenue and spending decisions in Congress, though the extent of this influence varies from year to year. It is usually the case that the president has far more influence when a majority of lawmakers in Congress are members of the president's own political party.

Step 2: The House and Senate Pass Budget Resolutions

Once the president's budget request has been released, Congress begins the months-long process of reviewing the request and laying out its own spending and taxation priorities. Generally, Congress adds funding in certain areas or for certain programs and reduces it in others. In theory, Congress could ignore the president's request entirely and start from scratch. As a practical matter, however, that rarely happens—in large part because no member of Congress has access to an accounting office like OMB, and therefore lacks the capacity to produce a comprehensive budget like the president's. Furthermore, all spending decisions made in Congress ultimately require the president's signature to become law. If Congress proposes funding for programs the White House opposes, the president can veto the bill, and the Congressional process starts over. Often the mere threat of a presidential veto is enough to get Congress to drop, or at least modify, offending provisions. If the president vetoes a bill, then a two-thirds majority in both the House and Senate is necessary to override the president; that requirement makes it just about impossible for Congress to get around a presidential veto.

After the president submits the budget request and lawmakers have thoroughly reviewed it, the **House Committee on the Budget** and the **Senate Committee on the Budget** each writes a **budget resolution**.[49] In this case, as with all spending and tax bills, the House writes its version before the Senate does.[50] A budget resolution is not a legally binding document; rather, it is more like a blueprint. It sets overall annual spending limits for federal agencies but does not set specific spending amounts for particular programs. After the House and Senate each pass a budget resolution, a joint **conference** comes together to iron out differences between the two versions, and a reconciled version then goes up for a vote in each chamber.[51] Conference means members of the House and Senate together reconcile two different versions of a piece of legislation.

Step 3: House and Senate Subcommittees "Markup" Appropriation Bills

The **Appropriations Committees** in both the House and the Senate are responsible for determining the precise levels of budget authority for all discretionary programs.[52] Recall from Chapter 2 that budget authority is the legal power of a federal agency to spend money by entering into obligations. The Appropriations Committees in both the House and Senate are then broken down into smaller **Appropriations subcommittees**, which review the president's budget request and the justification materials pertaining to the federal agencies under their specific jurisdictions. For example, there is an Appropriations subcommittee with jurisdiction over homeland security and another one for energy and water. After each subcommittee reviews the

What are Appropriations "Subcommittees"?

In both the House and the Senate, Appropriations subcommittees are smaller committees made up of members from the Appropriations Committee. Each of these subcommittees has jurisdiction over funding for a different area of the federal government. There are 12 different appropriations subcommittees.[53] The names and jurisdictions of these subcommittees, like the budget process as a whole, have evolved over time. Currently the 12 subcommittees are:

- Agriculture, Rural Development, and Food and Drug Administration
- Commerce, Justice, and Science
- Defense
- Energy and Water
- Financial Services and General Government
- Homeland Security
- Interior and Environment
- Labor, Health and Human Services, and Education
- Legislative Branch
- Military Construction and Veterans Affairs
- State and Foreign Operations
- Transportation, and Housing and Urban Development

president's request, it conducts hearings and poses questions to leaders of its associated federal agencies about each agency's requested budget.[54]

Based on all of this information, each subcommittee chair writes a first draft of the subcommittee's appropriations bill, abiding by the spending limits set out in the budget resolution. This first draft of the appropriations bill is called the chair's mark. All subcommittee members then consider, amend, and finally vote on the bill. Once it has passed the subcommittee, the bill goes to the full Appropriations Committee. The full committee reviews it, and then sends it to the full House or Senate for consideration.

The "Chair's Mark" and Majority Power

Subcommittee markups are perhaps the most critical step in the federal budget process. Before the markup begins, subcommittee chairs draft a document known as the chair's mark. It is the first draft of what the subcommittee—and later the whole Appropriations Committee and the full House or Senate—eventually will adopt. It covers every dollar for every agency and program that comes under the subcommittee's jurisdiction. In drafting the chair's mark, the subcommittee chair wields incredible power, making decisions about the life and death of federal programs.

Technically, other subcommittee members can add funding for programs after the chair has written his or her draft. As a practical matter, however, adding additional funding or funding a new program that is not in the chair's mark is tricky, since the chair's first draft usually doles out all the money allotted to the subcommittee in the budget resolution. This means that members seeking to add new funding will have to get a majority of the other subcommittee members to agree on removing funding somewhere else. This brings them into direct conflict with the chair.

So, how does a subcommittee member, or any House or Senate member, go about ensuring funding for a particular program? The best method is to get the funding included *in the chair's mark*. The chair knows this is the best strategy, and that makes her or him all the more powerful.

Subcommittee chairs have established processes for how they handle what are known as member requests, requests by other lawmakers for spending on certain things, which are known as **earmarks**. Earmarks are provisions added to legislation to designate money for very specific purposes.[55] Usually an earmark brings federal money into the state or congressional district of the lawmaker who requested the project. That's one way lawmakers try to guarantee that the federal budget serves their own constituents.

Subcommittee chairs generally specify a deadline for when such requests should be submitted to the chair. To the extent that chairs have resources available, they generally will include requests by subcommittee members first, usually of either party, to ensure future loyalty. The next priority is requests by members of the full Appropriations Committee, followed by requests from non-committee members. Requests by members of the chair's party leadership receive preferential treatment, often jumping to the front of the line, since decisions about who chairs which committees are controlled by senior members of the party. Requests from other members of a chair's home state also tend to get priority, regardless of party affiliation.

Since subcommittee chairs wield enormous power in the appropriations process—determining where billions of federal dollars will be spent—and since the majority party determines who will chair these subcommittees, the majority party has a strong hand in shaping federal spending. Of course, the president ultimately has to sign appropriations bills in order for them to become law, but the majority party in Congress has a great deal of power within that restraint.

What's more, the majority party has complete control over the House Committee on Rules—that's the committee that decides which bills the House will consider, and which it will not. That means the majority party not only shapes federal spending priorities, but it also exercises control over all legislative activity in the House.[56]

Step 4: The House and Senate Vote on Appropriations Bills and Reconcile Differences

The full House and Senate then debate and vote on appropriations bills from each of the 12 subcommittees. After both the House and Senate pass their versions of each appropriations bill—for example, each chamber passes a bill to fund Energy and Water—a conference committee meets to resolve differences between the House and Senate versions. After the conference committee produces a reconciled version of the bill, reflecting compromises made by members of each chamber, the House and Senate vote again, but this time on a bill that is the same in both chambers.[57] After passing both the House and Senate, each appropriations bill goes to the president.

All About Earmarks

The term earmark originally is a term from farming—it refers to the mark that farmers put on the ear of a cow or pig to mark ownership. But in federal budget parlance, an earmark is a provision added to legislation that diverts money from an agency's budget into a particular project, sometimes specifying the company, organization, or group of individuals who will receive a government contract to execute the project. Usually earmarks divert money into the congressional district of the lawmaker who added the provision to a piece of legislation. Earmarks are also called "pork-barrel" spending.

In recent years earmarks have received overwhelming negative attention and have come to symbolize what some people see as secretive and wasteful spending by lawmakers.

Numerous lawmakers who have publicly called for steep reductions in federal spending have been caught writing earmarks for bridges or military contracts in their home districts. Michelle Bachmann, representative from Minnesota, has spoken out against earmarks. But, she says, "There's a big difference between a teapot museum and a bridge over a vital waterway."[58] The difference may be in the eye of the beholder.

In fiscal year 2010, the lawmakers with the dubious distinction of sponsoring or co-sponsoring the most earmark spending are Senator Thad Cochran, a Republican from Mississippi who is the vice chairman of the Senate Committee on Appropriations, and Representative Mazie K. Horono, a Democrat from Hawaii. Rep. Hirono earmarked around $150 million in 2010, while Senator Cochran earmarked nearly half a billion dollars.[59]

Step 5: The President Signs Each Appropriations Bill and the Budget Becomes Law

The president must sign each appropriations bill after it has passed Congress for the bill to become law. When the president has signed all 12 appropriations bills, the budget process is complete. Rarely, however, is work finished on all 12 bills by October 1, the start of the new fiscal year.

Figure 4.3 puts all of the steps of the budget process into a diagram, so you can see how all the pieces fit together.

When the budget process is not complete by October 1, Congress passes a **continuing resolution** so that agencies continue to receive funding until the full budget is in place.[60] A continuing resolution extends funding until new appropriations bills become law.

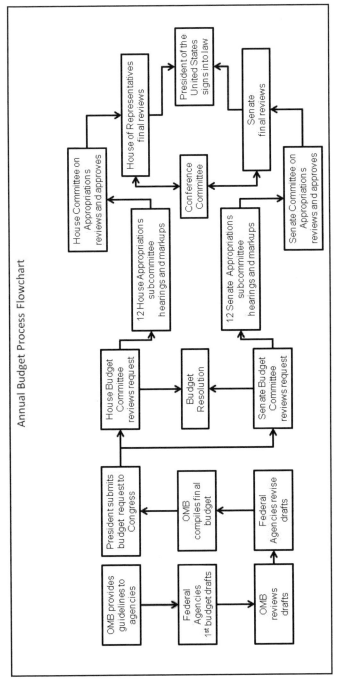

Annual Budget Process Flowchart

FIGURE 4.3

How the Federal Government Funds Emergencies

From time to time Congress has to respond to unanticipated situations for which there is no planned funding. For example, when Hurricane Katrina hit New Orleans in 2005, Congress passed a special bill to fund disaster relief. That kind of special legislation is called a **supplemental appropriation**.[61] Generally requested by the president, supplemental appropriations are enacted outside the normal budget process, usually in an expedited manner.

Sometimes lawmakers use supplemental appropriations as an opportunity to add extra money to funding for nonemergency programs. This can make it difficult for constituents to keep track of the total amount of funding that went to each federal program, since supplemental appropriations add money to funding that was appropriated during the regular appropriations process.

It's Even Messier than It Sounds

So far, this chapter has focused on the budgeting process as it is supposed to go. You might have thought it sounded pretty complicated—and it is. In practice, it's even *more* complicated than what you've already read. Politics, economics, and the efforts of lobbyists add considerable complications.

Political Ideology and Budget Priorities

Different political affiliations tend to correspond with different budget priorities, so there's nearly endless disagreement among lawmakers about the proper role for the federal government on any given issue. People on the right side of the political spectrum, known as conservatives, tend to believe that government should be as small as possible and that taxes have huge negative effects on the economy. These conservative beliefs tend to translate into less government spending and lower tax rates, with the general exception of military spending, which is usually a priority for those on the right. Meanwhile, people on the left side of the political spectrum, often known as liberals, tend to believe that the government must provide certain things, like robust social programs for the disadvantaged, and that any negative effects of taxes are outweighed by the value in providing government services. These liberal beliefs tend to translate into relatively more government spending and higher tax rates. In the middle of the spectrum are moderates, who do not espouse the typical conservative or liberal views, but fall somewhere in the middle.

In theory, Republicans are conservatives, and Democrats are liberals, but there are so many exceptions to this rule that it's difficult to pinpoint any defining set of characteristics about either party. Depending on the circumstances, both sides make a multitude of exceptions to their broad visions about the role of government. For example, President George W. Bush, who was widely considered to be a conservative and on the right of the political spectrum, presided over vast expansions in the size of the federal government over the course of his presidency.[62]

Lawmakers are likely to divert from their stated budget priorities when they see an opportunity for political gain (or to avoid a political defeat). For example, members of one party may oppose an initiative they normally would support just because the other party proposed it. Washington has been rife with this

There Are More than Two Political Parties

There are other political parties beyond the Democratic and Republican parties. These parties are called third parties. To name a few: the Green Party advocates for environmental health among other progressive issues, the Libertarian Party advocates for small government and individual rights, and the Working Families Party advances a pro-labor platform with a focus on economic and employment issues.

kind of partisan conflict in recent years, which has more than once arrested the budget process and nearly shut down the federal government. Chapter 8 explains recent budget strife in more detail.

Recently a new but unofficial political party has influenced politics in Washington. The Tea Party began to hold meetings and demonstrations in 2009, espousing a platform of lower taxes, less government spending, and less government debt. The Tea Party movement quickly attracted significant attention from media outlets and Washington lawmakers, and in the 2010 elections, candidates with Tea Party support won enough seats in the House to have an impact on the budget process. These "tea partiers," as they call themselves, wielded considerable power in the House largely because they voted in a bloc; that is, they worked together to support or oppose legislation, and working together they had enough influence to affect the passage of bills.[63]

Voting in a bloc is not a new strategy in Washington, and in fact there are official "caucuses" which are intended to do just that, when it comes to certain issues. For example there is a Congressional Progressive Caucus, a Congressional Black Caucus as well as a Women's Caucus.[64] There are numerous other caucuses dedicated to a host of different kinds of issues, and membership in a caucus sometimes can transcend party affiliation, such as when a lawmaker feels so strongly about a particular issue that she votes contrary to party line.

Economic Theory and Federal Budget Priorities

There are overarching economic goals that the government as a whole tends to strive for, including economic growth, full employment, and low inflation. These goals are especially important during recessions, though they are also important when the economy is strong.

The primary ways that the federal government influences the economy are through **fiscal policy** and **monetary policy**. Monetary policy involves influencing the supply of money as well as the level of interest rates in the economy. The Federal Reserve System, also known as the Fed, is responsible for US monetary policy. It operates independently of the president and Congress, in order to insulate the financial system from politics. And because monetary policy is conducted through the Fed, it does not affect the federal budget process.[65] Fiscal policy, however, refers to the tax and spending decisions made by Congress and the president in the federal budget; in other words, fiscal policy—and not monetary policy—is the focus of this book.

The problem is that different economic theories prescribe different roles for the federal government in keeping the economy strong. Furthermore, lawmakers of varying political affiliations tend to subscribe to conflicting economic theories—making for conflict in Washington about the best ways for federal tax and spending policy to strengthen the economy.

There are two major competing approaches to understanding the economy and the role of the federal government. Economists who subscribe to what's called the neoclassical tradition believe that individuals and businesses, acting through free markets, will always come up with the most efficient allocation of resources; thus, government intervention in the economy should be kept to the bare minimum.[66] That is, taxes and government spending should be reduced to the lowest levels possible to allow the more efficient private sector to allocate goods and services.

Closely related to neoclassical economics is supply-side economics. According to this view, the best way to a sound, growing economy is to support the ability of producers to produce—in other words, government policies should be geared toward creating optimal conditions for businesses, in order to encourage them to grow and hire more workers. That's what supply refers to—businesses *supply* the goods and services that consumers purchase. According to supply-side theory, the government should reduce regulations and taxes, thereby putting more money into the hands of businesses to encourage investment, job creation, and a better standard of living for everyone.[67]

In general, lawmakers who subscribe to neoclassical and supply-side economics tend to fall on the right side of the political spectrum. Senator Mitch McConnell, a Republican from Kentucky, has spoken out against Democratic lawmakers' proposals to raise taxes on wealthy Americans. McConnell argues that many of these wealthy Americans are business owners, and therefore higher tax rates would adversely affect job creation. Regarding the sluggish economy in 2011, Senator McConnell argued, "The Democrats' response to the jobs crisis we're in right now is to raise taxes on those who create jobs. This isn't just counterproductive. It's absurd."[68]

Neoclassical and supply-side theory, which often go hand in hand, are not the end of the story. A competing school of thought emphasizes *demand*-side policy; in other words, that federal tax and spending policies must help consumers, who spur the economy by *demanding* more goods and services and putting money into the cash registers of the businesses they patronize. According to this view, those businesses then turn around and hire more workers and produce more goods, because of the improved financial outlook that comes from having customers with money to spend.

This view was developed by John Maynard Keynes in the aftermath of the Great Depression in the 1930s. He argued that the central variable in the economy is demand and that no business will produce more goods or hire more workers in the absence of demand for its products.[69] Economists who follow Keynesian theory generally consider free markets to be efficient, but they also tend to believe that markets fail in ways that require government intervention. That is, the government sometimes should compensate for a shortfall in demand by doing things like cutting taxes for consumers, employing people directly, investing in infrastructure, or other such policies.

Those that argue for Keynesian-type policies are usually, though not exclusively, on the left side of the political spectrum. Many of President Obama's economic proposals have followed Keynesian theory; for instance, he has proposed cutting workers' payroll taxes, providing money to the states to retain teachers and firefighters who otherwise would be laid off, and hiring thousands of construction workers to repair roads and bridges. Keynesian theory suggests that this kind of government intervention will boost demand for goods and services throughout the economy because consumers will have more cash in their pockets.

Campaign Money

Nearly every lawmaker in Washington hopes to be re-elected, and running for re-election requires a lot of money. There is widespread fear that this need to raise campaign funds sways lawmakers' legislative priorities. In particular, many Americans fear that trade groups and other kinds of corporate interests have an opportunity to influence legislation by making large donations to members of Congress, who could return the favor by voting in donors' interests.[70]

In the 2010 election cycle, one one-hundredth of one percent of Americans (that's one in 10,000 people) contributed 24 percent of all the money donated by individuals to candidates, political parties, and political action committees (PACs).[71] The Federal Election Commission collects information about all political donors, including their professional occupation. The most common professions listed by these top-dollar donors were attorney, corporate executive, investor, and lobbyist.[72]

In 2010 the Supreme Court ruled on **Citizens United v. Federal Election Commission**, in a landmark decision that may substantially increase the role of money in politics. The Supreme Court ruled that corporations and unions have the right under the First Amendment to express political views. Previous campaign finance regulations had prevented corporations from running political advertisements within 60 days of an election, but those regulations were struck down by the court.[73] This decision opened the door to a vast new role for private entities to influence elections, with no limits on the amount of money they spend to do so. (There are limits on the amount of money individuals and corporations' PACs can give to candidates, but there is no limit on the amount of money corporations can spend on their own political advertising.)

Lawmakers' need to raise campaign funds also uses up a great deal of their time. Regardless of whether donors influence lawmakers' legislative priorities, it is certain that anyone elected to federal office must spend huge amounts of time calling and meeting donors and hiring a staff to do the same. That is time that is not spent on the business of governing.

Most Countries Have Publicly Financed Elections

The United States is unusual in that candidates for federal office generally must raise the money they need to pay for campaigning, which is very costly. Elected officials in most other countries receive public funds—that is, taxpayer money—to pay for campaign expenses. That means they do not need to spend the same time and resources to fundraise.[74]

Lobbying

Campaign donations go hand in hand with another force that makes federal budgeting still messier—**lobbying**. Lobbying refers to the act of trying to influence lawmakers, whether by organized groups of citizens, nonprofit organizations, or corporate trade groups.[75] The latter, trade groups, are responsible for the most widely known—and much maligned—kind of lobbying, in which corporations attempt to influence legislation, often to improve their profits. Trade groups, representing everything from health insurance companies to the telecommunications industry, often hire professional lobbying firms with expertise in influencing Congress.

According to the Center for Responsive Politics, in 2011 there were 12,242 registered lobbyists in Washington.[76] There are 535 members of Congress—100 in the Senate and 435 in the House—so that means there are 24 lobbyists for every lawmaker. It's much easier for lawmakers to hear the concerns of 24 lobbyists than the concerns of their every constituent. Representatives in the House serve districts that have an average population of 710,767, while senators represent entire states.[77] It's difficult or impossible for the population of an entire congressional district or state to organize behind particular issues or priorities the way that corporate interests with professional lobbyists do.

All Politics is Local

As former House Speaker Thomas P. "Tip" O'Neill was fond of saying, "All politics is local."[78] Indeed, while lawmakers in Washington face partisan disagreement, conflicting theories about how the federal budget can best help the economy, and a fire hose of requests from lobbyists and campaign donors, they also answer to voters back home in their districts and states. In other words, despite a multitude of barriers, many lawmakers are trying their best to serve the constituents who voted them into office.

And despite the power of lobbyists, the messiness of politics, and the complexity of the federal budget process, ultimately it is the American people who elect each and every member of Congress and the president. All people, thus, have a responsibility to pay attention to what elected officials are doing and to cast a vote during elections.

Chapter 9 explains a multitude of ways to get involved in order to ensure that your voice is heard by Congress.

1) The president releases a budget request every February for the coming fiscal year; that request officially is known as *the Budget of the United States Government.* However, the president's budget is *only* a request.

2) Congress uses the president's request as a starting point, after which lawmakers spend many months drafting 12 appropriations bills. Once all 12 of these bills have passed both the House and the Senate, and the president has signed them, the federal budget becomes law.

3) A host of forces add considerable complications to the federal budget process. A few of these forces are:
   • conflicting political ideologies
   • disagreement over how the economy works and how the government should try to influence the economy
   • campaign fundraising.

Appropriations Bills allocate funds to individual federal agencies. They specify how much money can be spent on a given program, and grant the government authority to enter into legal obligations that are later paid in outlays. Reviewed by the corresponding subcommittees of the appropriations committees in both the House and Senate, appropriations bills must also be approved by the full House and Senate before being signed by the president.

Appropriations Committees in both the House and the Senate are responsible for determining the precise levels of budget authority for all discretionary programs.

Appropriations Process is the annual process through which Congress creates the discretionary budget.

Appropriations Subcommittees in both the House and the Senate are committees made up of members of the full Appropriations Committee. Each of these subcommittees has jurisdiction over funding for a different area of the federal government. Currently there are 12 Appropriations subcommittees.

Authorization Bill gives a government agency the legal authority to fund and operate its programs. An authorization bill also sets maximum funding levels and includes policy guidelines. Government programs can be authorized on an annual, multiyear, or permanent basis. Specific amounts authorized serve as ceilings on the amounts of money that subsequently may be appropriated, though either the House or Senate may recommend appropriating lower amounts or nothing at all.

Budget Resolution is a resolution passed by each house of Congress that serves as a framework for budget decisions. It sets overall spending limits but does not decide funding for specific programs.

Citizens United v. Federal Election Commission is a Supreme Court case in which the court ruled that corporations and unions have the right under the First Amendment to express political views. This decision opened the door to a vast new role for private entities to influence elections, with no limits on the amount of money they spend to do so.

Conference refers to members of the House and Senate coming together to reconcile their two different versions of a given piece of legislation.

Continuing Resolution extends funding for federal agencies until new appropriations bills become law.

Earmarks are provisions added to legislation to designate money for a particular project, company, or organization, usually in the Congressional district of the lawmaker who sponsored it.

Fiscal policy refers to decisions made by the federal government regarding government spending and taxation.

House Committee on the Budget is the committee in the US House that is responsible for writing a budget resolution, among other responsibilities. It became a standing committee with the passage of the Congressional Budget and Impoundment Control Act of 1974.

Lobbying is the act of trying to influence lawmakers.

Monetary Policy refers to actions by the Federal Reserve Bank to influence the supply of money in the economy as well as interest rates.

Senate Committee on the Budget is the committee in the US Senate that is responsible for writing a budget resolution, among other responsibilities. It became a standing committee with the passage of the Congressional Budget and Impoundment Control Act of 1974.

Supplemental Appropriation is legislation that provides funding beyond what was appropriated in the normal appropriations process. Congress generally passes supplemental appropriations in response to emergencies like natural disasters or other kinds of urgent circumstances.

FIVE

Where Does the Money Come From?

"Taxes, after all, are the dues we pay for membership in an organized society."
—Franklin D. Roosevelt

"In this world nothing can be said to be certain except death and taxes."
—Benjamin Franklin

The federal government raises trillions of dollars in tax revenue each year, though there are many different kinds of taxes. Some taxes fund specific government programs, while other taxes fund the government in general. When all taxes for a given year are insufficient to cover all of the government's expenses, which is often the case,[79] the US Treasury borrows money to make up the difference.

Total federal tax revenue in fiscal year 2011 was $2.38 trillion.[80] Tax revenues come from three major sources: Income taxes paid by individuals, which accounted for 47 percent of all tax revenues in 2011; **payroll taxes** paid jointly by workers and employers, which were 36 percent; and corporate income taxes paid by businesses, making up 8 percent. There are also a handful of other types of taxes like customs duties and excise taxes that make up much smaller portions of federal revenue. Customs duties are taxes on imports, paid by the importer, while excise taxes are taxes levied on specific goods, like gasoline. Figure 5.1 illustrates how these different kinds of taxes contribute to overall tax revenues.

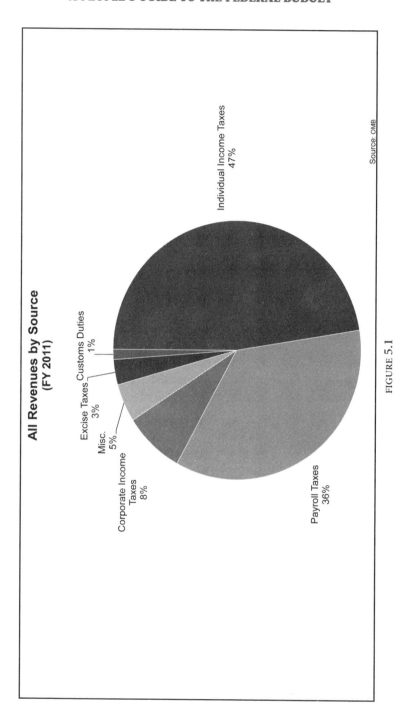

All Revenues by Source
(FY 2011)

Individual Income Taxes
47%

Payroll Taxes
36%

Corporate Income Taxes
8%

Misc.
5%

Excise Taxes
3%

Customs Duties
1%

Source: OMB

FIGURE 5.1

There's an Excise Tax for Bronzing Up at the Tanning Salon

There is a 10 percent excise tax on indoor tanning salon services. Effective July 1, 2010, the tax raises money to help pay for provisions of the Patient Protection and Affordable Care Act, the 2010 health care reform legislation.[81]

Once they are paid into the Treasury, income taxes and corporate taxes are designated as **federal funds**, while payroll taxes become **trust funds.** Federal funds are general revenues, meaning Congress and the president can decide to spend them on just about anything when they conduct the annual appropriations process described in Chapter 4. But trust funds can be used only for very specific things.

Income Taxes

More than 100 million American households file a federal income tax return each year, and those income taxes make up the federal government's single largest revenue source.[82] The income tax system is designed to be progressive, meaning that wealthy people are meant to pay a larger percentage of their earnings than low- or middle-income earners pay, though that is not always the way it works out.

Figure 5.2 shows the tax rates that apply to different income levels; these tax rates determine how much every American worker must pay in annual income taxes. These varying rates for different income levels are called **marginal tax rates**. A marginal tax rate is the rate at which your last dollar of income is taxed. So, for example, if you are single and you make $22,000 per year, then your first $8,500 of income is taxed at a rate of 10 percent, and the rest of your income is taxed at 15 percent.[83] In that case, 15 percent is your marginal tax rate. In total, you would owe around $2,875 in federal income taxes in 2011, before accounting for credits and deductions.

As you can see in Figure 5.2, there are six different marginal tax rates, and your marginal tax rate—the rate at which your last dollar of income is taxed—depends on how much you earn in a given year.

The Earned Income Tax Credit

The Earned Income Tax Credit (EITC) is a tax credit intended to make employment more rewarding for low- and middle-income wage earners. The EITC gives working people an extra boost in income.[84] To qualify for the credit, an individual or married couple must have earned income below a certain amount and file a federal tax return.[85] The EITC doesn't just reduce the amount of taxes owed; if a person qualifies for the EITC but owes no income taxes, then he gets a check in the mail from the federal government.

Similar to the EITC is the Child Tax Credit, which reduces the federal income taxes owed by parents by up to $1,000 per qualifying child.[86] This policy is intended to help working parents.

The Size of the Bush Tax Cuts

President George W. Bush lowered tax rates in 2001 and 2003, and those lower rates are reflected in Figure 5.2. Although the "Bush tax cuts," as they are called, apply to all income levels, they have been controversial because most of the benefits have gone to wealthy Americans. The wealthiest 5 percent saved more than $1 trillion in taxes in the decade since 2001 as a result of these tax cuts.[87] That's the same amount of money the federal government spent over the same decade on the Supplemental Nutrition Assistance Program (SNAP), commonly known as food stamps, the Special Supplemental Nutrition Program for Women, Infants, and Children (WIC), and all other food and agriculture programs combined.[88]

Since the federal government collects much of its annual tax revenue from income taxes, the amount of revenue it collects is different every year, depending on how much Americans earn in total. When the economy is strong and more people are employed, Americans earn more wages—and pay more in taxes. When the economy suffers, tax collections decline as well. In this way, federal revenues rise and fall with the economy.

Corporate Taxes

Corporations pay income taxes similar to those paid by workers. Depending on how much profit a corporation makes, it pays a marginal tax rate anywhere from 15 to 35 percent.[89] The top marginal tax rate for corporations, 35 percent, applies to taxable income over $18.3 million. As you can see in Figure 5.3, individual income taxes make up a much larger share of all federal revenues than corporate taxes do, in part because the wages and salaries of all Americans are much larger than profits of all US corporations.

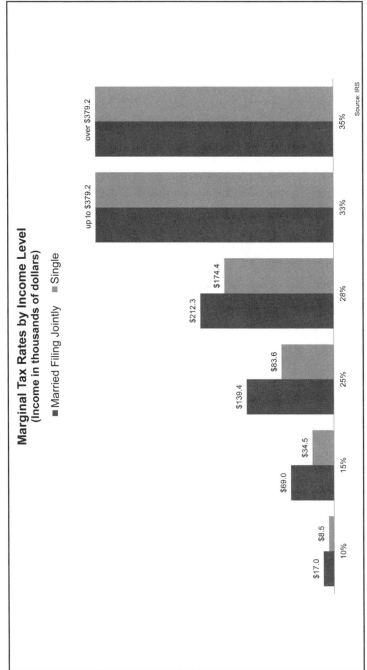

Marginal Tax Rates by Income Level
(Income in thousands of dollars)

■ Married Filing Jointly ■ Single

over $379.2

up to $379.2

$174.4

$212.3

$83.6

$139.4

$34.5

$69.0

$8.5

$17.0

10% 15% 25% 28% 33% 35%

Source: IRS

FIGURE 5.2

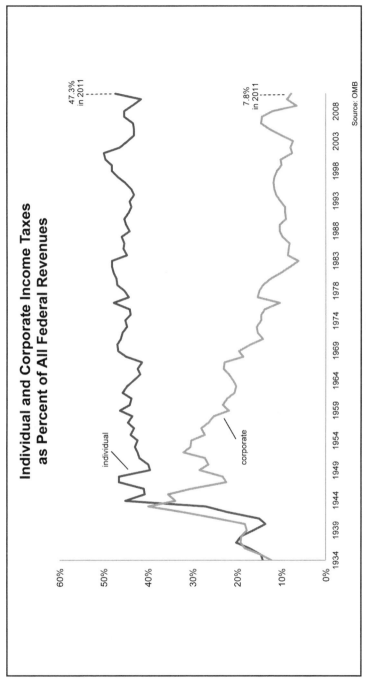

FIGURE 5.3

The Buffet Rule

Wealthy Americans pay most of the income taxes collected by the federal government each year. As you earn more money, you owe more in taxes, so the wealthiest people owe the most in taxes. However, while those wealthy earners pay larger sums of money than their middle-class counterparts, the amount they pay is often a smaller *percentage* of their incomes. That means the tax code sometimes works out to be **regressive**; that is, low-income people sometimes pay a higher effective tax rate than wealthy people.

According to the Congressional Research Service, around a quarter of all millionaires—94,500 taxpayers—pay a lower effective tax rate than 10.4 million "moderate-income" households, or those making less than $100,000 per year.[90] That prompted billionaire investor Warren Buffet famously to claim that he and other super-rich Americans pay too little in taxes.

You might ask how that's possible, since Figure 5.2 clearly shows that Americans must pay higher tax rates when they earn more money. But those tax rates apply to payroll wages—the money you take home in your paycheck. There are two other types of income that mostly go to the wealthy and are taxed at lower rates than payroll wages: "capital gains," which are profits earned from selling assets like real estate, and "dividends" earned from stocks.

Currently capital gains and dividends are taxed at a maximum rate of 15 percent.[91] That means taxpayers earning more than $34,500 per year in wages pay a higher marginal tax rate than millionaires earning all of their income from investments. This prompted President Obama to call for changes that would enforce the "Buffet Rule," the idea that millionaires should not pay a smaller share of their income in taxes than middle-class wage earners do. To date, Congress has not undertaken such changes.

While the official tax rate for most corporations is 35 percent, the **effective tax rate**—the percentage of profits a corporation *actually* pays in taxes—varies enormously from one corporation to the next.[92] That variation is the result of incredible complexity in the US tax code as well as corporations' varying exploitation of "loopholes" to avoid tax liability. "Loopholes" refer to provisions in the tax code that exempt certain activities from regular taxation. For example, multinational corporations can shift US profits to overseas operations and reduce their tax liability by doing so.

Even corporations earning the same amount of profit, or corporations within the same industry, often pay wildly different effective tax rates. For example, between 2008 and 2010, FedEx earned $4.2 billion in profits and paid an average tax rate over those years of less than one percent.[93] Its competitor, the United Parcel Service, earned $12.4 billion from 2008 to 2010 but paid on average 24 percent of those profits in taxes.[94] Such a vast difference is not unusual in the world of corporate taxes.

The Tax Code Plays Favorites

Lawmakers frequently use the tax code to encourage certain activities. For example, homeowners effectively receive a **subsidy** for home ownership, because they can deduct mortgage interest from their tax liability. A subsidy is direct assistance from the federal government to individuals or businesses, which lessens the cost of certain activities. In the case of the home-mortgage interest deduction, which effectively is a subsidy, home ownership is less expensive than it would be without that special tax deduction. That means the government gives preferential treatment to homeowners over renters. There are many other kinds of subsidies in the tax code which affect individuals and corporations in countless ways.

While corporations' tax avoidance strategies usually are legal, the tax code is rife with loopholes in large part because of lobbying efforts by those corporations. In other words, corporations spend money in efforts to influence lawmakers, because those lawmakers have the power to alter the tax code in ways that reduce corporations' tax burden.[95]

History of Federal Fund Revenues

The US Constitution (Article I, Section 8) grants Congress the power to collect taxes. Early federal taxation was mostly in the form of excise taxes on goods such as alcohol and tobacco. Although a tax on personal income existed briefly during the Civil War, it wasn't until 1913, with the ratification of the 16th Amendment to the Constitution, that income taxes became permanent. Subsequently, the

Do We Tax Corporations a Lot or a Little?

A hotly debated issue is how much the federal government should tax corporations. Some people argue that the US taxes corporations more heavily than do other industrialized nations and therefore we should cut corporate tax rates. Other people say we tax corporations at *lower* rates than other countries, so we should raise taxes. Who is right?

Both are right in different ways, actually. The *official* marginal tax rate for US corporations is one of the highest in the world. But loopholes make *effective* tax rates much lower than those of peer nations. Overall, the Congressional Budget Office found that corporate taxes as a percentage of GDP are lower in the US than in nearly every other developed nation.[96] Figure 5.4 shows how the US stacks up compared to taxes on corporate profits in other developed nations.

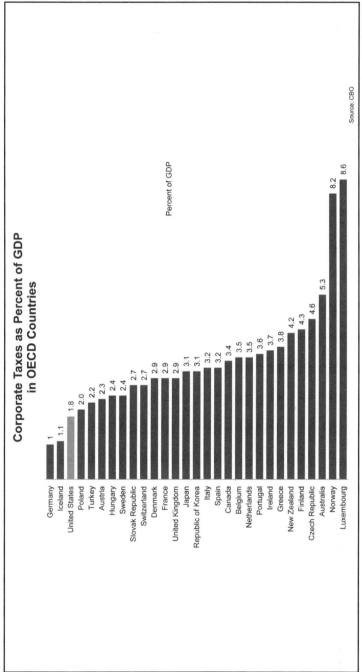

Corporate Taxes as Percent of GDP in OECD Countries

Percent of GDP

Source: CBO

FIGURE 5.4

tax code grew more complicated with the addition of exemptions, deductions, tax credits, and other kinds of tax policies.

Figure 5.2 illustrates current income tax brackets and how marginal tax rates rise as income increases. As you can see, currently there are six tax rates corresponding with six different income brackets; the lowest marginal tax rate applies to income up to $8,500, while the highest rate applies to all income over $379,151. Imposing just six tax brackets is very different from historic income tax policy. In the past there were well over a dozen different tax brackets.

Figure 5.5 shows the tax brackets for a single person in 1955; notice that income over $200,000 (in 1955 dollars) was taxed at 91 percent. In other words, for every dollar of income over $200,000 that a single person earned in 1955, he gave 91 cents to the federal government. By comparison, today's income tax system is far less progressive, as the wealthiest earners keep a far greater share of their income than they used to. The system is also far less *graduated*, meaning that we do not gradually phase in a spectrum of increasing marginal tax rates in the same manner that we did in 1955.

Corporate tax rates also have changed over time. As noted above, effective tax rates currently paid by corporations vary widely and typically are far lower than the official rate of 35 percent. Both official and effective corporate tax rates have

1955 Single		
Marginal Tax Rate	Tax Brackets Over	But Not Over
20.0%	$0	$2,000
22.0%	$2,000	$4,000
26.0%	$4,000	$6,000
30.0%	$6,000	$8,000
34.0%	$8,000	$10,000
38.0%	$10,000	$12,000
43.0%	$12,000	$14,000
47.0%	$14,000	$16,000
50.0%	$16,000	$18,000
53.0%	$18,000	$20,000
56.0%	$20,000	$22,000
59.0%	$22,000	$26,000
62.0%	$26,000	$32,000
65.0%	$32,000	$38,000
69.0%	$38,000	$44,000
72.0%	$44,000	$50,000
75.0%	$50,000	$60,000
78.0%	$60,000	$70,000
81.0%	$70,000	$80,000
84.0%	$80,000	$90,000
87.0%	$90,000	$100,000
89.0%	$100,000	$150,000
90.0%	$150,000	$200,000
91.0%	$200,000	-

FIGURE 5.5

TAX BRACKETS IN 1955[97]

Earnings Statement

Company Name
0000 Nonexistent Ave.
Nowhere, USA 00000

Pay Period: 1/01/2012 to 1/15/2012
Pay Date: 1/20/2012

John Doe
0000 Any St.
Nowhere, USA 00000

Hours and Earnings			Taxes and Deductions	
Hours	**Rate**	**Earnings**	**Description**	**Amount**
100	$10.00	$1000.00	Federal _These are your federal income taxes._	$250.00
			State	$160.00
			Social Security _These are state taxes._	$42.00
			Medicare	$14.50
			These are your federal payroll taxes, also known as FICA.	
Gross Year-to-Date	**Gross This Pay Period**		**Total Deductions**	**Net Pay**
$1000.00	$1000.00		$466.50	$533.50

FIGURE 5.6 FEDERAL TAXES ON YOUR PAYSTUB

declined over the past century. In 1950, corporations paid an average effective tax rate over 50 percent; by 2005, that number had fallen below 30 percent, where it hovers today.[98, 99]

Payroll Taxes

While individual and corporate income taxes are designated as federal funds, as described above, payroll taxes are designated as trust funds. Trust funds can be used only for very specific purposes, mainly to pay for **Social Security** and **Medicare**. Social Security, officially called the Old Age, Survivors, and Disability Insurance program, is meant to ensure that elderly and disabled people do not live in poverty. Medicare is a federal program that provides health care coverage for senior citizens and the disabled.

Taxes to finance Social Security were established in 1935 as a payroll deduction—these are the payroll taxes you see taken directly out of your paycheck, labeled on pay stubs as Social

Do Some People Pay No Taxes at All?

Sometimes you hear people say, "Half of all Americans pay no taxes," or something along those lines. Indeed, because many people do not earn enough to owe federal income taxes, and because of deductions and credits like the Earned Income Tax Credit, many Americans end up paying no income taxes, or even pay negative income taxes; that is, they receive a check from the US Treasury.

But that doesn't mean they pay no taxes. That's because *all* wage earners, regardless of income level, contribute to Social Security and Medicare. In fact, more than half of all taxpayers pay more in payroll taxes than they do in income taxes.[100] Furthermore, all people pay federal excise taxes when they buy gasoline, cigarettes, and a host of other items. Like the Social Security tax, these excise taxes are regressive, because working-class people spend a far greater share of their incomes on consumer goods than do their wealthier counterparts. (The excise tax on cigarettes draws criticism for being particularly regressive, since those who spend a significant slice of their income on cigarettes tend to earn very modest incomes.)

Security and Medicare taxes or as "FICA." FICA stands for the Federal Insurance Contributions Act, the law that mandates funding for Social Security through a payroll deduction. Figure 5.6 shows how FICA appears on a typical paycheck. (This paycheck is meant merely to illustrate how federal income taxes and FICA are itemized on a paystub. The numbers are not meant to represent actual rates.)

The Social Security tax is regressive, meaning that low-income taxpayers pay a greater share of their income to Social Security than their wealthier counterparts do. That's because Social Security taxes currently apply only to the first $110,100 of wages.[101] The Medicare tax, however, applies to all wages, and therefore is not regressive but *proportional*, meaning all wage earners pay the same share of their income to Medicare. However, neither the Social Security nor the Medicare tax applies to non-wage income, so wealthy individuals who earn all of their income from investments do not have to pay FICA.

The deductions from your paycheck are only half the story of payroll taxes. Employees and employers *each* pay 6.2 percent of wages into Social Security and 1.45 percent into Medicare. That means your employer deducts 7.65 percent of your wages from your paycheck to contribute to those programs, and then your employer contributes an equal amount, though you never see documentation of your employer's contribution.

Currently there is a payroll-tax holiday in effect, so workers pay 4.2 percent of their wages as payroll taxes instead of 6.2 percent. This was part of lawmakers' efforts to stimulate the economy during its slow recovery from the Great Recession; at the end of 2012, workers once again will pay 6.2 percent of wages.

Borrowing

In most years, the federal government spends more money than it takes in from tax revenues. To make up the difference, the Treasury borrows money by issuing bonds. Anyone can buy Treasury bonds, and, in effect, lend money to the Treasury by doing so. In fiscal year 2011, the federal government borrowed around $1.3 trillion, or around 36 percent of all revenues that year. Borrowing, therefore, constitutes a major source of revenue for the federal government. Down the road, however, the Treasury must pay back the money it has borrowed, and pay interest as well. (See Chapter 7 for more on deficits and debt.)

1) The major sources of revenue for the federal government are individual income taxes, corporate income taxes, and payroll taxes. Individual and corporate income taxes are designated as federal funds, and the president and Congress decide how to spend that money every year in the appropriations process. Payroll taxes become trust funds, money that is set aside for Social Security, Medicare, and other social insurance programs.

2) Individual income taxes are the single largest source of federal revenue. The income tax system is designed to be progressive, meaning that wealthy people are meant to pay a larger percentage of their earnings than low- or middle-income earners pay, though that is not always the way it works out.

3) Corporations pay income taxes the way individuals do, though corporate income taxes make up a significantly smaller revenue source than individual income taxes. The official marginal tax rate for corporations is 35 percent, but effective corporate tax rates tend to be much lower.

Effective Tax Rate is the percentage of income an individual or corporation actually pays in taxes. Effective tax rates often differ from official tax rates due to tax credits, deductions, or loopholes in the tax code.

Federal Funds are funds collected by the federal government for general purposes, as opposed to trust funds, which are collected by the federal government for specific purposes.

Marginal Tax Rate is the rate at which your last dollar of income is taxed. So, for example, if you are single and you make $22,000 per year, then your first $8,500 of income is taxed at a rate of 10 percent, and the rest of your income is taxed at 15 percent. In that case, 15 percent is your marginal tax rate.

Medicare is a federal program that provides health care coverage for senior citizens and the disabled. It is funded through payroll taxes.

Payroll Taxes are taxes paid jointly by employers and employees. Payroll taxes fund the Social Security and Medicare programs.

Progressive refers to a tax system in which wealthier people pay a higher percentage of their income in taxes than lower-income people. Progressive also describes political ideology on the left side of the political spectrum.

Regressive refers to a tax system in which people earning lower incomes pay a higher percentage of their income in taxes than their wealthier counterparts.

Subsidy refers to direct assistance from the federal government to individuals or businesses, which helps defray the costs of certain activities.

Trust Funds are funds collected by the federal government for specific purposes, as designated by law. For example, payroll taxes are trust funds collected by the federal government to pay for the Social Security and Medicare programs.

SIX

Where Does the Money Go?

"A billion here, a billion there—sooner or later
it adds up to real money."
—Attributed to Senator Everett Dirksen

In fiscal year 2011, the federal government spent $3.73 trillion. These trillions of dollars make up a considerable chunk—24 percent—of US Gross Domestic Product (GDP). That means that federal government spending makes up a sizable share of all money spent in the United States each year. So, where does all that money go? This chapter looks at all of the money the federal government spent in 2011. You'll see lots of different ways of looking at outlays from the 2011 fiscal year; recall from Chapter 2 that outlays are actual expenditures. In this chapter, you'll see outlays broken down into many categories, from mandatory and discretionary, to total outlays, to outlays as percent of GDP.

How Big Is One Trillion Dollars?
If you earned $1 million every year it would take you one million years to earn $1 trillion.

Figure 6.1 shows how the different sources of tax revenue described in Chapter 5 are grouped into federal funds and trust funds, and then spent on a host of different kinds of programs. As Figure 6.1 illustrates, individual and corporate income taxes as well as some smaller revenue sources are designated as federal funds after they're

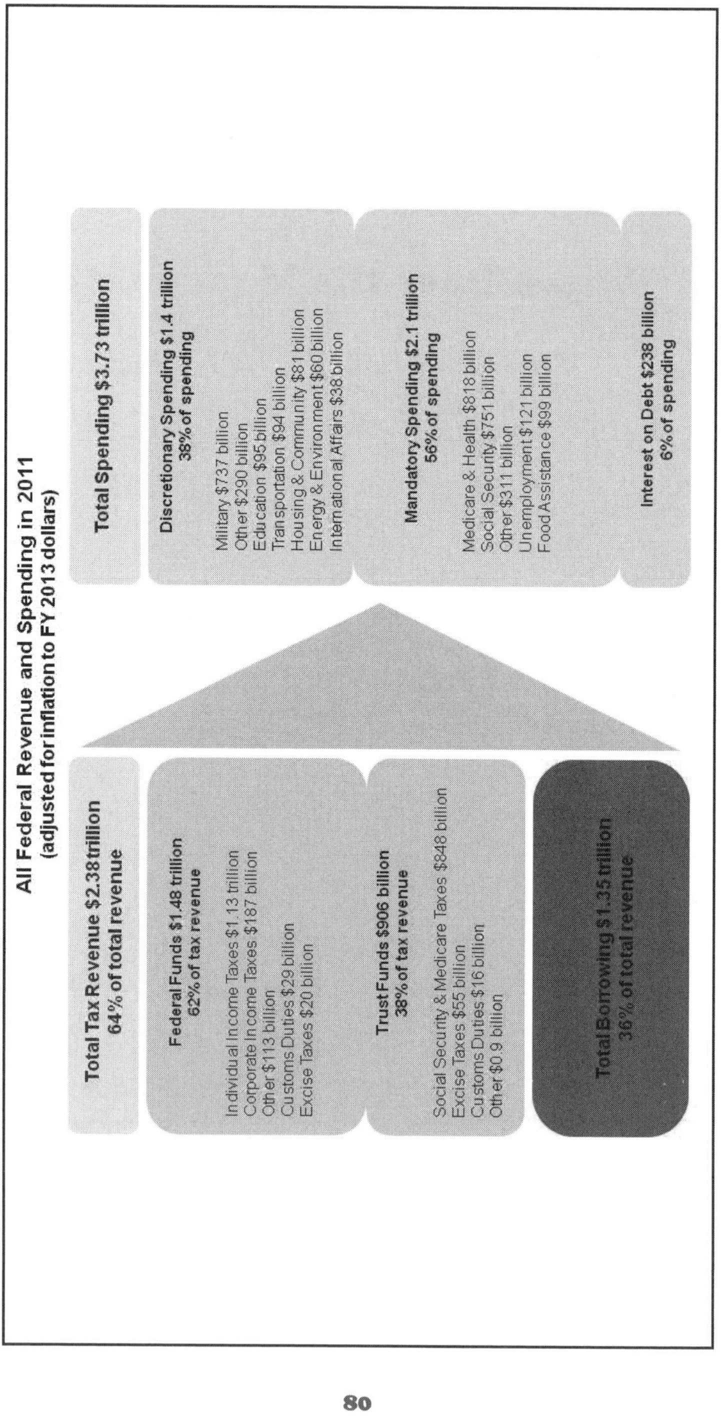

All Federal Revenue and Spending in 2011
(adjusted for inflation to FY 2013 dollars)

Total Tax Revenue $2.38 trillion
64% of total revenue

Federal Funds $1.48 trillion
62% of tax revenue

Individual Income Taxes $1.13 trillion
Corporate Income Taxes $187 billion
Other $113 billion
Customs Duties $29 billion
Excise Taxes $20 billion

Trust Funds $906 billion
38% of tax revenue

Social Security & Medicare Taxes $848 billion
Excise Taxes $55 billion
Customs Duties $16 billion
Other $0.9 billion

Total Borrowing $1.35 trillion
36% of total revenue

Total Spending $3.73 trillion

Discretionary Spending $1.4 trillion
38% of spending

Military $737 billion
Other $290 billion
Education $95 billion
Transportation $94 billion
Housing & Community $81 billion
Energy & Environment $60 billion
International Affairs $38 billion

Mandatory Spending $2.1 trillion
56% of spending

Medicare & Health $818 billion
Social Security $751 billion
Other $311 billion
Unemployment $121 billion
Food Assistance $99 billion

Interest on Debt $238 billion
6% of spending

FIGURE 6.1

paid into the Treasury; federal funds accounted for 62 percent of all tax revenues in 2011. Payroll taxes combine with a few much smaller revenue sources to become trust funds, and those accounted for 38 percent of all tax revenues. Together, federal funds and trust funds—all taxes paid into the Treasury—accounted for 64 percent of all money spent by the federal government, and the rest came from borrowing. The Treasury then used those trillions of dollars of tax revenue and borrowed funds to pay for all federal programs— everything from military operations in Afghanistan to lunches for children in schools across the country.

Figure 6.2 presents another way of looking at where the federal government spends trillions of dollars, with all federal spending broken into an array of categories, the largest of which is Social Security, Unemployment & Labor. Indeed, in every year for decades, Social Security has constituted a sizeable chunk of federal spending, while unemployment benefits have grown especially large in recent times, in the wake of the Great Recession. Medicare & Health is the second largest category, followed by Military. Interest on Debt, much smaller than military spending, is the fourth largest kind of spending.[102]

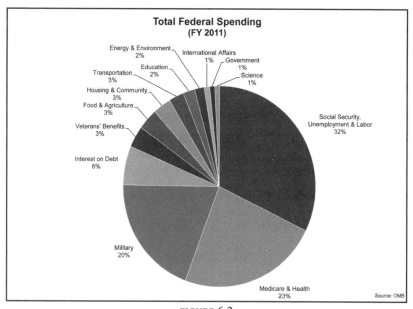

FIGURE 6.2

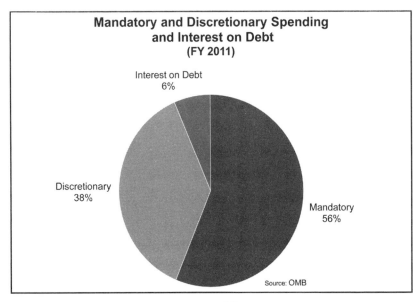

FIGURE 6.3

Mandatory and Discretionary Spending

The US Treasury divides all spending into three groups: **mandatory spending, discretionary spending**, and **interest on debt.** Interest on debt, which is much smaller than the other two categories, is the interest the government pays on its accumulated debt, minus interest income received by the government for assets it owns. Figure 6.3 shows all federal spending in 2011 broken into these three categories.

Discretionary spending refers to the portion of the budget that goes through the annual appropriations process described in Chapter 4. In other words, Congress directly sets the level of spending on programs that are discretionary; members of Congress can choose to increase or decrease spending on any of those programs in a given year during the appropriations process.

Even though it does not represent the largest share of federal spending, the discretionary budget often is the one that receives the most scrutiny from individuals and the media and the most attention from lobbyists who want to influence federal spending. That's because the discretionary budget changes each year at the discretion of lawmakers, making it subject to the influence of

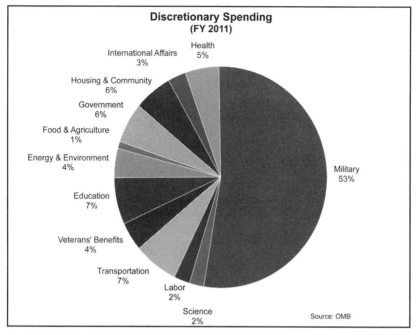

FIGURE 6.4

engaged citizens, the special-interest groups and lobbyists described in Chapter 4, and newsworthy to media outlets that want to report on government spending.

Figure 6.4 shows all discretionary spending in fiscal year 2011. Military spending made up the largest share of the discretionary budget, accounting for 53 percent in 2011. Other types of discretionary spending are Education (7 percent), Health (5 percent), and Housing & Community (6 percent).

Mandatory spending, also called direct spending, is spending that is not determined through the annual appropriations process but rather by the eligibility or payment rules of certain programs. Congress writes authorizing legislation stating that certain people are eligible for benefits from federal programs like food stamps— officially called the Supplemental Nutrition Assistance Program (SNAP)—and thereafter food stamps are awarded to anyone who meets the stated eligibility criteria. Federal spending on food stamps therefore is called mandatory spending because anyone who is eligible and applies for benefits must, by law, receive those benefits.

The Politics of Measuring Federal Spending

The requested federal budget for fiscal year 2013 is $3.67 trillion. Or, more specifically, $3,667,076,000,000. That's a lot of money, and any number so big can be broken apart and categorized in a lot of different ways. The federal budget is also very political—it represents the priorities of lawmakers and constituents, the outcome of countless lobbying efforts, and the livelihoods of millions of people.

For all of these reasons, different organizations with varying political motives choose to measure and categorize the federal budget in a host of different ways, and those differences often serve a political or ideological agenda. That means that when you see a graph or chart about federal spending, you should take note of the person or organization that produced it. For example, some people will choose only to present the discre-

tionary budget, or the mandatory budget, or the total budget. As you've learned, discretionary, mandatory, and total spending are all quite different, and they're all important pieces of the budget puzzle. So it's important to pay attention to precisely which numbers you are reading and to recognize that the information may be presented in a particular way in order to serve a political purpose.

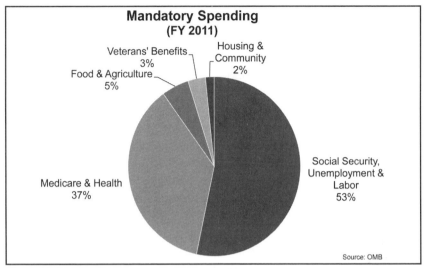

FIGURE 6.5

Congress, therefore, cannot decide each year to increase or decrease the budget for food stamps, the way it can for discretionary programs. Instead, it periodically reviews the eligibility rules and may change them in order to exclude or include more people.

As you can see in Figure 6.3, mandatory spending makes up more than half of total federal spending. By far the largest mandatory program is Social Security, which by itself constituted more than one-third of mandatory spending and 20 percent of all federal spending in 2011. Medicare is the next largest mandatory program. Figure 6.5 breaks down mandatory spending into categories. (While some mandatory spending occurs in categories not included in Figure 6.5, such as Military, the amounts are so small as to be less than 1 percent of all mandatory spending, and thus they are omitted from Figure 6.5.)

Because of the nature of mandatory spending, which includes programs like food stamps and unemployment benefits, it naturally increases when the economy falters. In an economic downturn, more people are unemployed and qualify for need-based assistance. The converse is also true; as the economy rebounds, mandatory spending declines as fewer people require federal assistance. See "Helping People and the Economy" for more on the economic impact of these need-based programs.

Helping People and the Economy

In an economic downturn, the federal government automatically spends more on benefits such as food stamps and unemployment compensation, because more people qualify for those programs. These programs are meant to help Americans make ends meet through tough times.

But these programs serve another purpose besides helping those in need. During a recession, lawmakers look for ways they can help get the economy back on track—generally by increasing spending or cutting taxes, both of which are intended to stimulate extra economic activity. Food stamps and unemployment benefits do exactly that; they give the economy a boost, because the low-income people who receive those benefits quickly turn around and spend the money they receive. That extra spending means grocery stores and other establishments put more money into their cash registers than they would have otherwise and, therefore, can retain workers they might have laid off or even hire new workers. These workers receive paychecks, and they turn around and spend *that* money, and so on, to create a ripple of extra economic activity, called the **multiplier effect**, that started with federal spending.[103] Eventually, as the economy improves, fewer people need federal benefits, and the economy doesn't need government stimulus.

Another way that lawmakers often help people and the economy during an economic downturn is by cutting tax rates. Tax cuts function in much the same way as federal spending on food stamps and unemployment benefits; they put extra money in the pockets of regular people, who spend more money as a result. "Economic Theory and Federal Budget Priorities" in Chapter 4 has more about how the federal budget influences the economy.

Tracking Your Income Tax Dollar

Another way of looking at how the federal government spends money is to track where your federal income tax dollars go. That's different from measuring discretionary spending or total spending, because your income tax dollars go exclusively into federal funds, which are spent differently from trust funds. Recall from Chapter 5 that federal funds are tax revenues that can go toward any government program, but trust funds can be used only for very specific things.

Are Federal Funds the Same as Discretionary Spending?

It would be easy to assume that federal funds simply become discretionary spending, since by definition federal funds can be used to fund any government function, and discretionary spending is the spending determined each year at the discretion of lawmakers. However, federal funds do not directly correspond with discretionary spending. Referring to Figure 6.1, you will notice that federal funds make up 62 percent of all revenues, while discretionary spending is 38 percent of all federal spending. In other words federal fund revenue is much greater than discretionary spending and therefore, a great deal of federal funds pay for mandatory spending.

Figure 6.6 shows a breakdown of where your 2011 federal income tax dollars went (or your parents' or guardians' income tax dollar, if you don't yet pay taxes). In other words, Figure 6.6 shows where all federal funds were spent in 2011.

As you can see from Figure 6.6, more than a quarter of every income tax dollar goes to the military. Other significant chunks pay for Medicare & Health and Interest on Debt.

Some people think the federal government should write them a receipt for their income tax dollars to show exactly what the government bought with the money. Figure 6.7 does just that.

History of Federal Spending

The federal government has not always spent trillions, or even billions, of dollars every year. Prior to the twentieth century, the federal government spent far less than it does currently (even in inflation-adjusted terms) because many of the major government programs that exist today, such as Social Security and Medicare,

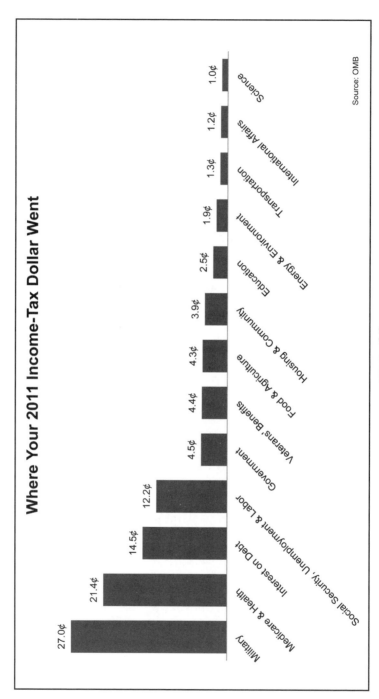

Where Your 2011 Income-Tax Dollar Went

Military	27.0¢
Medicare & Health	21.4¢
Interest on Debt	14.5¢
Social Security, Unemployment & Labor	12.2¢
Government	4.5¢
Veterans' Benefits	4.4¢
Food & Agriculture	4.3¢
Housing & Community	3.9¢
Education	2.5¢
Energy & Environment	1.9¢
Transportation	1.3¢
International Affairs	1.2¢
Science	1.0¢

Source: OMB

FIGURE 6.6

Federal Income Tax Receipt

April 15, 2012
Thank you for your business!

Military $716.01
Includes $18.12 for nuclear weapons

Medicare & Health $567.38
Includes 3¢ for Maternal, Infant and Early Childhood Home Visiting Programs

Social Security & Labor $323.13
Includes $15.73 for Temporary Assistance for Needy Families

Housing & Community $103.23
Includes $9.34 for disaster relief

Government $119.54
Includes 84¢ for the postal service

Food & Agriculture $113.00
Includes $71.37 for SNAP (food stamps)

Veterans Benefits $115.82
Includes $9.70 for rehabilitation, education, and job training for veterans

Education $65.53
Includes 40¢ for the Corporation for Public Broadcasting

Energy & Environment $51.25
Includes $6.19 for energy conservation

Transportation $34.43
Includes 28¢ for High Speed Rail

International Affairs $32.08
Includes 28¢ for the Global Fund to Fight AIDS, Tuberculosis, and Malaria

Science $27.10
Includes $15.66 for space flight research

Interest on Federal Debt $385.49

Total federal income taxes   ***$2,654***

Have a nice day!

FIGURE 6.7

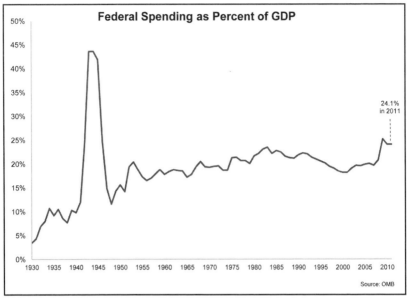

FIGURE 6.8 (THIS FIGURE ALSO APPEARS IN CHAPTER 3 AS FIGURE 3.3)

had not yet been created. Throughout US history, however, the budget has expanded rapidly during wartime. For example, in 1861 just prior to the Civil War, federal spending totaled $66.5 million dollars (in nominal terms). By the end of the war just four years later, government spending by the Union had risen to nearly $1.3 billion—almost a 2,000 percent increase—and 89 percent went to the Department of War and the Navy Department.[104]

Similarly, in 1916 and prior to US involvement in World War I, total federal spending was less than $750 million in nominal terms, but it grew to $18.5 billion in 1919, an increase of over 2,500 percent. (Only nominal figures are available for these historical numbers.) Over 95 percent of total spending in that year was related to war costs.[105] During World War II, federal spending nearly hit 45 percent of GDP, which remains its historical high since record keeping began in the 1930s.[106] Figure 6.8 shows federal spending as a percent of GDP since 1930.

After World War II, federal spending declined dramatically, but it did not return to pre-war levels. In the mid-1950s, federal spending rose again, driven in part by benefits for veterans such

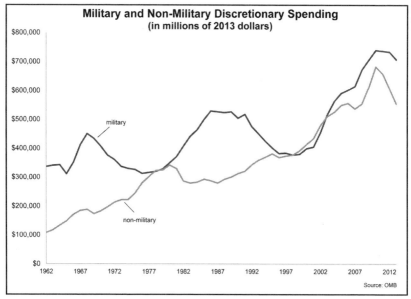

FIGURE 6.9

as those mandated in the GI Bill, the legislation that funded college tuition and vocational training for veterans.

Then, in 1964, President Johnson began what he called the War on Poverty, a response to steep poverty rates across the country that affected people of color disproportionately.[107] Johnson's efforts, dubbed the "Great Society," created new federal programs aimed at helping low-income Americans. Many of the programs that began during this era have become cornerstones of the modern social-safety net, including the food stamp program and Medicare and Medicaid, which provide health care for millions of elderly and low-income Americans. (See "Extra! Major Social Programs Funded in the Federal Budget" at the very end of this chapter for more on these and other programs.)

In the 1980s, President Reagan presided over increases in military spending in response to the Cold War. This constituted a shift in national priorities, from the social programs of President Johnson's era to President Reagan's expanded militarism. Figure 6.9 illustrates this shift, dividing all discretionary spending into military and nonmilitary spending. You can see the jump in the military's share of discretionary spending in the 1980s.

In the 1990s under President Clinton, federal spending declined. In 1996 new welfare reform laws dramatically changed the way the federal government assists low-income families. Between 1993 and 1999, the number of welfare recipients in the US declined by 7.5 million people, or 53 percent,[108] as a result of these policy changes.[109] Federal spending on welfare declined substantially as a result.[110]

Federal spending increased dramatically under President George W. Bush, as the United States entered wars in Iraq and Afghanistan. Together the two wars cost the federal government more than $1.2 trillion by the end of 2011.[111] Other kinds of spending also increased under President Bush. He presided over the creation of a prescription drug benefit as part of the Medicare program, which increased the already growing cost of Medicare.[112]

In 2009 as President Obama took office, federal spending reached 25 percent of GDP, its highest point since World War II, as Figure 6.8 illustrates. This growth was the result of sharp spending increases intended to buoy the economy after the Great Recession. The American Recovery and Reinvestment Act of 2009 provided $780 billion for public works projects, tax cuts, and expansions of need-based programs.[113] Mandatory spending

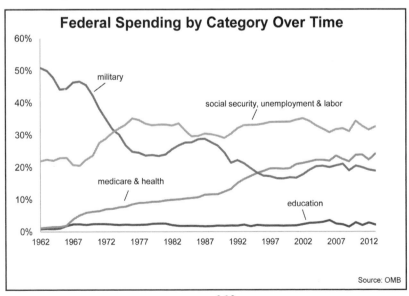

FIGURE 6.10

ballooned during the Recession, as more and more Americans who were hard hit by the weak economy qualified for unemployment benefits, food stamps, and other kinds of assistance. The federal government also spent billions of dollars on the Troubled Asset Relief Program (TARP) during this time, in response to the mortgage crisis that contributed to the Great Recession. TARP was intended to help financial institutions overcome the plummeting value of financial assets that were tied to home values across the country. (Much of the money the federal government loaned to banks as part of TARP was later repaid.[114])

As federal spending has grown over time, the *composition* of spending has changed as well; that is, the programs requiring the largest share of the federal budget have shifted. For example, spending on health care has taken up an increasingly large portion of all spending, from one percent in 1962 to around 24 percent in 2011. Figure 6.10 shows how four different categories of spending have ebbed and flowed as a percent of total federal spending over time.

For more history on the federal budget, see Chapter 3.

Budget Trade-Offs

When making budgetary decisions, it isn't just the monetary cost—the cost in dollars—that lawmakers and constituents must take into consideration. Resources are finite, and wants are infinite. That means everything included in the federal budget forces something else to be omitted. Thus, when choosing what to buy with our tax dollars, we have to consider the opportunity cost in addition to the monetary cost. An **opportunity cost** is what you give up when you make a choice, measured in terms of the next best alternative.

A typical example is going to college. If it costs, say, $15,000 per year to go to college, the cost for four years of college education is $60,000. But in making the decision to go to college, you forego the opportunity to work and earn a wage during those four years. Perhaps you'd expect to earn $20,000 in each of those four years. That means the opportunity cost of going to college is $80,000. Rather than strictly thinking about the cost of tuition when deciding whether or not to attend college, you also should consider the opportunity cost.

This is part of the reason why many budget decisions are so contentious. For example, many people believe military spending is a vital priority for the nation's tax dollars, and thus we should cut other kinds of spending when necessary in order to make sure that the military has everything it needs. Critics of this view say that the opportunity cost of cutting other kinds of spending is too high, arguing that funding for things like scientific research provides valuable long-term benefits, and thus should not be cut to pay for military programs.

The trade-offs inherent in the federal budget have consequences that extend all the way down to the local level. For example, in 2008 the federal government spent $481.4 billion on the base budget for the Department of Defense.[115] The city of Colorado Springs, Colorado, paid about $1.35 billion in individual income taxes that year,[116] about $214 million of which went to the Department of Defense. For that same amount of money, Colorado Springs could have provided Head Start education for all 5,257 three- and four-year-olds in that city whose family incomes qualified them for Head Start enrollment;[117, 118] plus Colorado Springs could have paid for health insurance for its 10,717 uninsured children;[119, 120] plus it could have awarded the maximum Pell grant to every college student residing there;[121] and it would have had enough left over to hire 1,656 teachers for kindergarten through twelfth grade.[122]

1) Federal spending is divided into three broad categories: mandatory and discretionary spending, and interest on the federal debt.

2) Mandatory spending for programs like Social Security and Medicare makes up more than half of all federal spending. Mandatory spending does not go through the annual appropriations process the way discretionary spending does; rather, levels of mandatory spending are determined by the eligibility rules of certain programs. Since more people are eligible for mandatory programs during poor economic times, mandatory spending naturally expands during recessions and contracts when the economy recovers.

3) Discretionary spending is the part of the budget that is subject to the annual appropriations process described in Chapter 4, and makes up around one-third of all federal spending each year.

4) Federal spending has increased over time, as new programs have been added to the activities of the federal government. While federal spending has increased, the composition of spending has also changed.

Interest on Debt is the interest payments the federal government makes on its accumulated debt, minus interest income received by the government for assets it owns.

Multiplier Effect is an economics term for an increase in national income that is greater than the initial increase in spending that caused it.

Opportunity Cost is what you give up when making a decision, measured in terms of the next best alternative.

Poverty Line, also called the poverty level or threshold, is determined by annual income. For example, the poverty line for a family of four was $22,113 in 2010; any family of four earning that amount or less was considered to be in poverty.

Major Social Programs Funded in the Federal Budget

The numbers on how much the federal government spends on many of these programs in your own state, and how funding is projected to change in 2013 relative to 2012, are available in Appendix: Federal Spending in the States.

FOOD STAMPS
(see **Supplemental Nutrition Assistance Program**)

HEAD START
Year founded: 1965[123]
Enrollment: 904,153 children in 2009[124]
What it does: Gives grants to agencies that provide early math and reading skills, as well as social and cognitive development opportunities, to low-income children.[125]
How recipients qualify: Any child who is five years old or younger and whose family is below the **poverty line** is eligible to apply for Head Start and Early Head Start services.[126] The federal poverty line, also called the poverty level or the poverty threshold, is determined by annual income. For example, the poverty line for a family of four was $22,113 in 2010; any family of four earning that amount or less was considered to be in poverty.

LOW INCOME HOME ENERGY ASSISTANCE PROGRAM
Year founded: 1981
Enrollment: 5.4 million in fiscal year 2008[127]
What it does: Gives low-income households assistance with energy costs. This can include heating assistance, cooling assistance, and home repairs that will help reduce energy costs. Assistance can be in the form of monthly benefits or crisis grants.[128, 129]
How recipients qualify: Eligibility is largely determined at the state level, but federal guidelines state that individuals earning less than 150 percent of the poverty level can be eligible. States are allowed to set additional restrictions, such as mandating that the household pass an assets test or have a utility disconnection notice.[130]

MEDICAID
Year founded: 1965[131]
Enrollment: 60 million in 2009[132]
What it does: Jointly funded by the federal government and the 50 states, Medicaid provides health insurance for low-income children and their parents, as well as pregnant women, and people with disabilities. In some states Medicaid also provides health insurance for low-income adults who do not have children.[133, 134]
How recipients qualify: The federal government sets eligibility at or below 133 percent of the poverty line for pregnant women and children, though states have considerable discretion over setting their own eligibility rules.[135]

MEDICARE
Year founded: 1965[136]
Enrollment: 47 million in 2010[137]
What it does: Provides health care for any person over the age of 65, and any person who has kidney failure or long-term kidney disease, and people who are permanently disabled, regardless of income.[138]

How recipients qualify: Those who are over the age of 65 or disabled qualify for Medicare.

NATIONAL SCHOOL LUNCH PROGRAM
Year founded: 1946[139]
Enrollment: 31.7 million children in 2010[140]
What it does: Gives cash reimbursements to schools or childcare facilities who supply low-cost or free lunches to children each school day.[141, 142]
How recipients qualify: Children whose households are at 130 percent of the poverty line or lower can receive free lunches. Children whose households are between 130 and 185 percent of the poverty line can receive reduced price lunches.[143]

PELL GRANTS
Year founded: 1972
Enrollment: 5.8 million students at the start of the 2011–2012 school year[144]
What it does: Provides need-based grants to undergraduate and vocational students. The maximum grant currently is $5,550 per year, though the precise award depends on full-time status, financial need, and length of time the student plans to attend school.[145]
How recipients qualify: Any undergraduate without a bachelor's degree who completes a Free Application for Federal Student Aid (FAFSA), demonstrates financial need, is a US citizen or qualifying noncitizen, and has a high school diploma or GED is eligible.[146]

SECTION 8
Year founded: 1974[147]
Enrollment: 3.3 million families in 2005 (the most recent number available)[148]
What it does: Subsidizes rent and utilities for very low-income families. There are two types of Section 8 funding.

One is the Housing Choice Voucher Program that allows families to find a private landlord from whom to rent. The other is project-based, meaning the family lives in housing projects specifically set aside for Section 8 recipients.[149, 150]

How recipients qualify: Eligibility is based on income and family size. Families' income may not exceed 50 percent of the median income for the county or city in which they live, and 75 percent of vouchers must go to those whose income does not exceed 30 percent of the median income. Because availability of Section 8 housing is limited, families are placed on a waiting list once they are deemed eligible.[151]

SOCIAL SECURITY

Year founded: 1935[152]

Enrollment: 54 million beneficiaries in 2010[153]

What it does: Provides cash benefits to retirees, the disabled, as well as the spouses, children, and dependent parents of workers who have died.[154]

How recipients qualify: Eligibility is based on year of birth or disability status. The dependents of deceased workers are also eligible for Social Security benefits.[155]

SPECIAL SUPPLEMENTAL PROGRAM FOR WOMEN, INFANTS, AND CHILDREN (WIC)

Year founded: 1972[156]

Enrollment: 8.9 million in 2011[157]

What it does: Provides low-income women who are pregnant or have children up to age five with food vouchers, health care referrals, and nutrition education. It is not an entitlement program, meaning every eligible woman does not receive assistance.[158, 159]

How recipients qualify: States determine precise eligibility. According to federal guidelines, states must set the qualifying income between 110 and 185 percent of the poverty line. The applicant also must obtain a referral from a physician, nurse, or nutritionist who determines that she or her children are "nutritionally at risk."[160, 161]

State Children's Health Insurance Program
Year founded: 1997[162]
Enrollment: 7.7 million children in 2010[163]
What it does: Provides health insurance to low-income children whose families earn too much money to qualify for Medicaid but cannot afford private health care.[164]
How recipients qualify: States may either provide benefits to children of families with incomes below 200 percent of the poverty level, or up to 50 percentage points above the state's current Medicaid income limit.[165]

Supplemental Nutrition Assistance Program (SNAP), formerly food stamps
Year founded: 1964 (though earlier versions of the program have existed since 1936)[166]
Enrollment: 45 million people in 2011[167]
What it does: Provides low-income people with cash benefits that can only be spent on food.[168, 169]
How recipients qualify: Individuals and families must earn below an income level that is different depending on how many people are in the household. For example, a household of two people must make below $1,226 per month to qualify, and they can receive a maximum monthly benefit of $367.[170]

Temporary Assistance for Needy Families (TANF)
Year founded: 1996 (though previous versions have existed since 1935)[171]
Enrollment: 4.4 million families in 2010[172]
What it does: Provides cash assistance to low-income families.[173]

How recipients qualify: States have flexibility in setting eligibility rules, but the state must ensure that half of the low-income families receiving TANF work at least 30 hours per week (or 20 hours for single parents). A family cannot receive benefits for more than 60 months.[174]

UNEMPLOYMENT INSURANCE
Year founded: 1935[175]
Enrollment: 7.3 million workers per week as of December 2011[176]
What it does: Provides cash benefits to laid-off workers. Benefit levels are calculated based on a percentage of the worker's last wages.[177]
How recipients qualify: Unemployment Insurance is available to workers who lost their job without fault and are actively seeking employment.[178]

WIC
(See Special **Supplemental Program for Women, Infants, and Children**)

SEVEN

The Federal Debt

*"A national debt, if it is not excessive,
will be to us a national blessing."*
—Alexander Hamilton, First US Secretary of the Treasury

Earlier chapters discussed revenues and government spending, which together comprise the annual federal budget. If these are equal in a given fiscal year, the government has a **balanced budget**. If revenues are greater than spending, the result is a **surplus**. But if government spending is greater than tax collections, the result is a **deficit**. The federal government then must borrow money to fund its deficit spending.

The **federal debt** is the total amount of money that the federal government has borrowed over the years to finance its deficits, minus what it has since repaid. (The federal debt is also called the national debt.) Every year the government runs a deficit, the money it borrows adds to the federal debt. Therefore, the federal debt is the sum of all past deficits. Contrarily, if the government runs a surplus, that allows the government to pay down some of its debt. That's just like when a person has some extra cash and uses the money to pay down credit card debt.

Why Do We Borrow?

The size of a budget deficit in any given year is determined by two factors: the amount of money the government spends in a given year and the amount of revenues the government collects in taxes during the same year. Both of these factors are affected by the state of the economy as well as by the tax and spending decisions made in the appropriations process described in

Chapter 4. For example, Congress may decide to repair interstate highways and bridges, both of which would increase government spending. Or Congress may reduce tax rates, thereby reducing total tax collections. Such decisions affect the size of the deficit or surplus.

As discussed in Chapter 6, during economic downturns government spending automatically increases because there is an upsurge in the number of people eligible for need-based programs. At the same time, revenues tend to decrease because fewer people are employed, and therefore federal income tax collections decline. Corporations also earn less profit and subsequently pay less in taxes. All of these factors increase the likelihood of budget deficits during a recession.

Lawmakers may also intentionally increase government spending during a recession, even though they know that the result will be a budget deficit. Recall from Chapter 4 that a major school of economic thought, called Keynesianism, suggests the government should use fiscal policies to stimulate demand when the economy is in a slump. For example, the government may increase spending on infrastructure, which would create jobs, or pass tax cuts to help workers. Another school of economic thought, supply-side economics, suggests that the government should lower corporate and investment taxes to encourage businesses to hire new workers and invest in new projects. The use of all of these kinds of fiscal policies is likely to create a deficit if the government is also facing reduced revenues.

Figure 7.1 shows budget deficits as well as occasional surpluses for every year since 1940. The black bars show the size of the deficit or surplus for each year, while the dark gray bars show the size of revenues and the light gray bars show the size of outlays. The deficit or surplus is just the difference between revenues and outlays in each year.

How Does the Federal Government Borrow?

To finance the debt, the US Treasury sells bonds and other types of securities.[179] Securities is a term for a variety of financial assets. Anyone can buy a bond or other Treasury security directly from the Treasury through its web site, http://www.treasurydirect.gov,

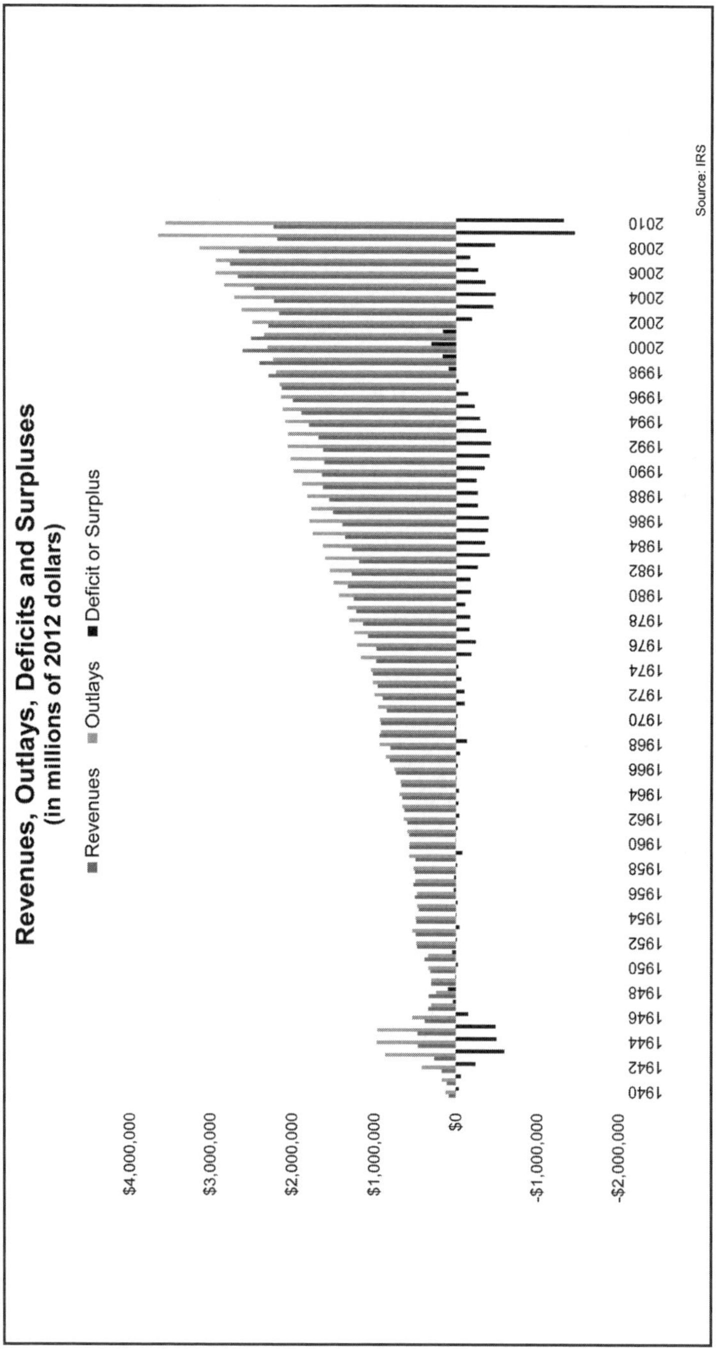
Revenues, Outlays, Deficits and Surpluses
(in millions of 2012 dollars)
Revenues
Outlays
Deficit or Surplus
$4,000,000
$3,000,000
$2,000,000
$1,000,000
$0
-$1,000,000
-$2,000,000
1940
1942
1944
1946
1948
1950
1952
1954
1956
1958
1960
1962
1964
1966
1968
1970
1972
1974
1976
1978
1980
1982
1984
1986
1988
1990
1992
1994
1996
1998
2000
2002
2004
2006
2008
2010
Source: IRS

FIGURE 7.1

or from banks or brokers. When a person buys a Treasury bond, she effectively loans money to the federal government in exchange for repayment with interest at a later date.

Most Treasury bonds give the investor—the person who buys the bond—a pre-determined fixed interest rate. Generally, if you buy a bond, the price you pay is less than what the bond is worth. That means you hold onto the bond until it matures; a bond is mature on the date at which it is worth its face value. For example, you may buy a $100 bond today and pay only $90. Then you hold it for five years, at which time it is worth $100. You also can sell the bond before it matures.

There are actually many different kinds of Treasury bonds, but the common thread between them is that they represent a loan to the Treasury, and therefore to the US government. As citizens of a democracy, Americans collectively own the federal government; thus a big portion of the federal debt—the portion that was leant to the government by regular Americans—is actually money that we owe to ourselves!

History of Federal Deficits

Over the past few years, there have been growing concerns over the fact that the federal government is running large budget deficits. By reading the newspaper, you might think that deficits and debts are new phenomena. However, that is far from the case. In the vast majority of years since 1900, the federal budget was in deficit. In fact, there were surpluses in only 31 out of 111 years since 1901, as you can see in Figure 7.2. The longest period of surplus budgets occurred in the 1920s during an extended economic boom.[180]

During World War II, the government deficit increased nearly ninefold through the height of the war as spending to fund the war effort dramatically increased.[181] During the postwar boom as soldiers returned home to work and wartime production converted back to domestic production, the country ran small surpluses.

In the 1980s, deficits increased under President Ronald Reagan as a result of his fiscal policies, which included reductions in individual and corporate income tax rates and expanded military spending in support of the Cold War with the Soviet Union.

In the mid to late 1990s, the US ran budget surpluses under President Bill Clinton, largely due to increases in tax rates for wealthy individuals and corporations, and unexpected revenues from a booming economy, in which stock market gains and rising incomes from the "dot com" bubble contributed to total revenues.

Under President George W. Bush's policies, projected surpluses were converted to deficits through rebates to taxpayers, the Bush tax cuts, the wars in Iraq and Afghanistan, and spikes in domestic security spending after September 11, 2001.

How Big Is the Federal Debt?

In 2011 the federal debt was $14.7 trillion, or around $47,000 for every US citizen.

A weak economy and President Obama's fiscal policies have increased the size of the deficit in recent years. To combat the Great Recession, the American Recovery and Reinvestment Act of 2009, commonly known as the "stimulus" or "stimulus package," provided over $780 billion in tax cuts, entitlement program extensions, and federal contracts and grants in order to stimulate the economy.[182] Lower tax revenues and expanded enrollment of need-based programs like unemployment insurance and Medicaid also contributed to rising deficits during the recession and the economy's slow recovery.

History of the Federal Debt

In 1791 during the Revolutionary War, the federal debt was around $75 million in nominal dollars, or 37 percent of GDP. During the Civil War, the level of nominal debt grew from $65 million in 1860 (1.5 percent of GDP) to $2.7 billion following the war (27 percent of GDP).[183] During World War II, the federal debt rose from 42 percent to 109 percent of GDP, as the government spent vast sums of money on the war effort.[184] Figure 7.3 shows federal debt as a percent of GDP since 1940.

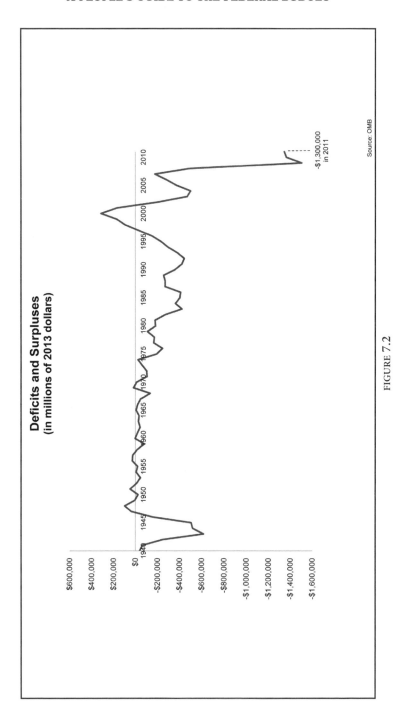

Deficits and Surpluses
(in millions of 2013 dollars)

-$1,300,000
in 2011

Source: OMB

FIGURE 7.2

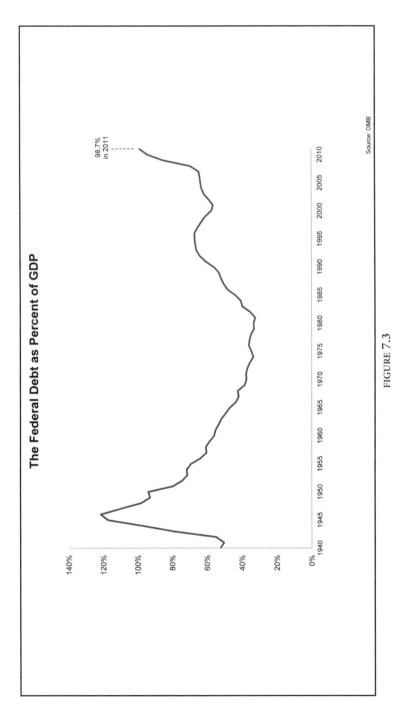

FIGURE 7.3

Why Measure the Federal Debt as a Percent of GDP?

It is a standard practice to measure the federal debt (the total amount owed by the federal government) in relation to GDP (the total income in the economy) in order to compare the debt across years. This ratio provides a snapshot of the financial health of the economy at a given time by showing the size of the financial burden—that is, government debt—relative to the whole economy.

Another measure is real federal debt, which takes nominal debt—that is, debt expressed in the current year's dollars—and then adjusts it for inflation. To compare the dollar value of the debt over different years, debt from each year must be converted into the same year's dollars. (For more on adjusting for inflation, see Chapter 2.) However, this measure can overemphasize the size of the current debt in relation to past years because it ignores the size of the economy. Thus, when you see the federal debt expressed in inflation-adjusted dollars instead of as a percent of GDP, beware that the author may be trying to exaggerate the size of the debt relative to historic levels.

For example, these two measures tell very different stories when comparing debt in 1946 and 2009. Federal debt was 121.7 percent of GDP in 1946, versus 85.2 percent in 2009, as you can see in Figure 7.4. However, the federal debt rose from $2.7 trillion in 1946 to $12.7 trillion in 2009, as you can see in Figure 7.5. So was the debt larger in 1946 or 2009? If you are referring to the size of the debt in dollars, then it was clearly larger in 2009. But if you want to know in which year the debt burden on the country was greater, then clearly the answer is 1946.

	Real Federal Debt (in 2013 dollars)	Federal Debt as a Percent of GDP
1946	$2.7 trillion	121.7 percent
2009	$12.7 trillion	85.2 percent

FIGURE 7.4 FEDERAL DEBT IN DOLLARS AND AS PERCENT OF GDP

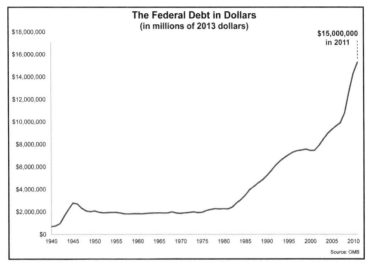

FIGURE 7.5

The only time in United States history in which there was *zero* federal debt was in 1835 under President Andrew Jackson. Skeptical of the power of the central bank (which today is called the Federal Reserve Bank), Jackson eliminated it and returned its assets to the US Treasury, which created a surplus great enough to pay off all federal debt at the time.[185] However, shortly thereafter the federal government began accumulating millions of dollars of new debt.[186]

Who Lends Money to the Federal Government?

Previously this chapter explained that much of the federal debt is owned by the American people, because we lend money to the federal government when we buy bonds and other Treasury securities. The total federal debt is the sum of the debt held by the public—

that's the amount the government has borrowed from regular Americans as well as from foreign entities—and **debt held by federal accounts**. Debt held by federal accounts is the amount of money that the Treasury has borrowed from itself. That may sound funny, but recall from Chapter 5 that trust funds are federal tax revenues that can only be used for certain programs. When trust fund accounts run a surplus, the Treasury takes the surplus and uses it to pay for other kinds of federal spending. But that means the Treasury must pay that borrowed money back at a later date. That borrowed money is what's called debt held by federal accounts. One-third of the federal debt is debt held by federal accounts, while two-thirds of the federal debt is held by the public.[187]

Debt Held by the Public

Debt held by the public is the total amount the government owes to all of its creditors in the general public. That includes Americans as well as foreign individuals and the governments of foreign countries.[188]

Approximately half—the largest portion—of debt held by the public is held internationally by foreign investors and central banks of other countries who buy our Treasury bonds as investments. In 2010, the countries that held this international portion included China, which held the most ($1.1 trillion), followed by Japan ($800 billion), Middle Eastern countries ($173 billion), Russia ($168 billion), Brazil ($164 billion), and Taiwan ($152 billion).[189]

The next largest portion is held by domestic investors, which includes regular Americans as well as institutions like private banks. (For example, a bank may invest some of its assets in Treasury bonds.) This portion constitutes over a third of the federal debt.

The Federal Reserve Bank and state and local governments hold the remainder of the federal debt. Each of these groups holds less than 10 percent. The Federal Reserve's share of the federal debt is not counted as debt held by federal accounts, because the Federal Reserve is considered independent of the government. The Federal Reserve buys and sells Treasury securities as part of its policies to control the money supply and set interest rates in the economy.

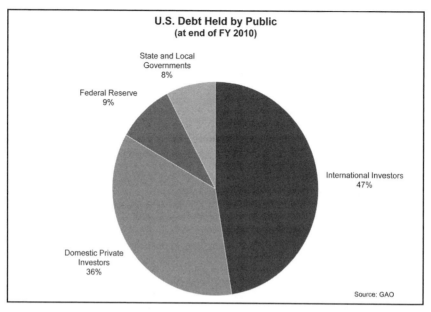

FIGURE 7.6

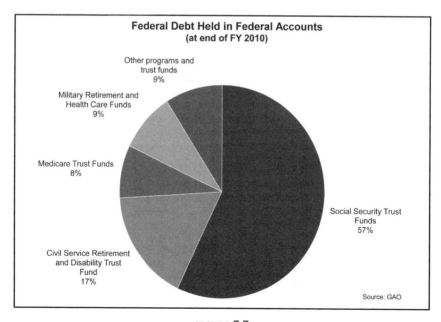

FIGURE 7.7

Debt Held by Federal Accounts

Debt held by federal accounts is the debt that the federal government has borrowed from itself. Trust funds, such as Social Security, Medicare, and the Civil Service Retirement Trust Fund, own most of that debt. In other words, the Treasury must pay back borrowed money with interest into those trust funds at some point in the future.[190]

When a trust fund account runs a surplus, the Treasury invests the surplus in Treasury bonds or other Treasury securities. The Treasury does this for a number of reasons. First, it enables the federal government to use trust fund surpluses to finance current spending. But another reason is that Treasury bonds earn interest with very low risk, so it's a way for trust fund surpluses to earn a return over time, just the way you might invest your own savings in a Treasury bond or other interest-bearing investment.[191]

EXTRA!

Does the Federal Debt Affect You?

The main reason to care about the size of the federal debt is that the government must spend billions of dollars every year on interest payments.[192] Just like a personal credit card, the larger the debt, the larger the interest payments. These payments are an opportunity cost of holding debt, which means that if the government did not have to make these interest payments, it would have that money to spend on critical government programs. Figure 7.8 shows interest on debt as a percent of all federal spending over the last half century.

Interest rates also affect the size of the interest payments the federal government must make on the federal debt. When interest rates are high, the Treasury sells bonds that pay a higher return, and thus the required interest payments rise. Currently, interest rates are low, which helps to keep down the total interest owed. However, when interest rates rise in the future, the required payment will increase.

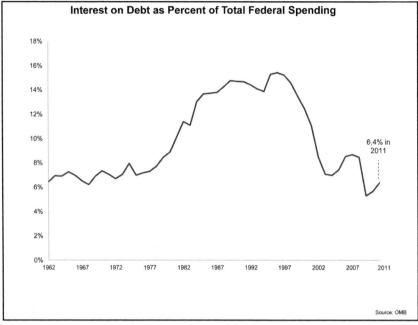

FIGURE 7.8

The Debt Ceiling

The **debt ceiling** is the legal limit set by Congress on the total amount that the US Treasury can borrow. If the level of debt hits the debt-ceiling limit, the government cannot borrow additional funds, potentially triggering a government shutdown and a default on existing loans. Congress has the legal authority to raise the debt ceiling as needed.

The debt ceiling was initially set in 1917 and has been raised 78 times since then, including 11 times since 2001.[193, 194] In most years, the decision by Congress to raise the limit is a simple procedure. As Figure 7.9 shows, Congress has voted to raise the debt ceiling on almost an annual basis over the past decade, and in some cases even more than once a year. However, in the midst of debates over the size of the federal budget and the role of deficit spending, and because of political partisanship, the debt ceiling has become extremely contentious and politicized, as occurred during the 2011 debt-ceiling debate. (See Chapter 8 for more on 2011 and the debt ceiling.)

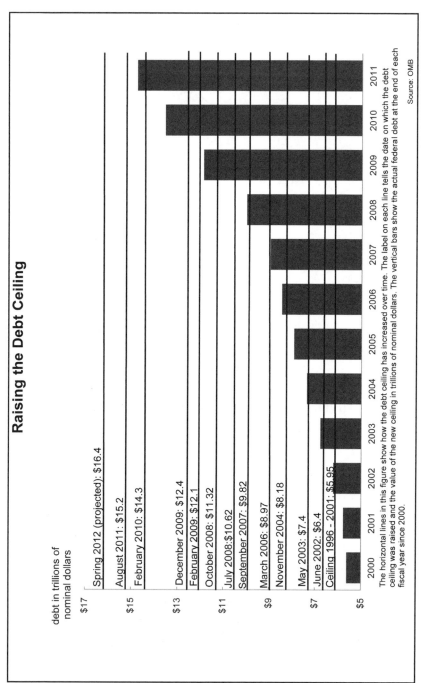

Raising the Debt Ceiling

debt in trillions of nominal dollars

Spring 2012 (projected): $16.4

August 2011: $15.2

February 2010: $14.3

December 2009: $12.4

February 2009: $12.1

October 2008: $11.32

July 2008: $10.62

September 2007: $9.82

March 2006: $8.97

November 2004: $8.18

May 2003: $7.4

June 2002: $6.4

Ceiling 1996 - 2001: $5.95

The horizontal lines in this figure show how the debt ceiling has increased over time. The label on each line tells the date on which the debt ceiling was raised and the value of the new ceiling in trillions of nominal dollars. The vertical bars show the actual federal debt at the end of each fiscal year since 2000.

Source: OMB

FIGURE 7.9

EXTRA!

BIG NEWS!

Are Deficits Bad?

There is an ongoing debate as to whether the government should limit its ability to borrow. Some consider deficit spending to be a hindrance to the government and the economy, arguing that a deficit only shifts the burden to future generations because it must be paid for eventually, just like any other loan.

Others see deficits as a crucial way for the government to stimulate the economy during an economic downturn. Proponents of this view believe that the role of government is not only to provide services that the private sector doesn't, but also to use fiscal policies to stimulate the economy during economic crises. They argue that deficits are necessary in times of economic hardship, but that during economic booms, budget surpluses should be used to pay down the debt.

Limiting or Eliminating Federal Deficits

There have been numerous attempts over the last 30 years to control deficits and shrink the federal debt. Many of these attempts have revolved around mandating a balanced budget, in which the government cannot spend more than its revenues in any given year and, thus, is prohibited from running deficits.

During the mid-1980s, the Balanced Budget and Emergency Deficit Control Act of 1985, also known as Gramm-Rudman-Hollings, set annual deficit targets with the goal of a balanced budget by FY1991.[195] This legislation required that if the annual targets were not met, then **sequestration**, or automatic spending cuts, would go into effect.

In 1986, the US Supreme Court declared Gramm-Rudman-Hollings unconstitutional on the grounds that it violated the separation of powers, since it gave the legislative branch the authority to execute a law—in this case, the automatic spending cuts—which is a power reserved for the executive branch. A revised bill was passed in 1987, known as Gramm-Rudman-Hollings II, which corrected this problem by transferring the sequestration authority to OMB, which is part of the White House. That legislation also raised the debt ceiling limit and postponed the balanced budget requirement.[196]

The Budget Enforcement Act, which was passed in 1990 and expired in 2002, provided an alternative approach to deficit reduction. Its intention was to control congressional actions by setting annual caps on discretionary spending and establishing pay-as-you-go (PAYGO) rules for taxes and entitlement programs. The PAYGO rule required new tax and spending legislation to be deficit-reducing or deficit-neutral—which meant that any new spending or reduced tax rates had to be offset by cutting spending or raising taxes elsewhere.[197]

After the 1994 midterm elections in which the Republicans gained control of the House of Representatives, Congress and President Clinton's sparring over the budget and deficits resulted in budget impasses and two government shutdowns. In 1995, congressional Republicans attempted to pass a Balanced Budget Amendment to the Constitution. In 1997, Congress and the White House passed the Balanced Budget Act, which set caps on discretionary spending and required sequestration if spending exceeded those limits.[198]

In fiscal years 1998 through 2001, President Clinton and Congress balanced the budget and ran a surplus. From 2002 onwards, deficits returned, as the Bush tax cuts returned the surplus to taxpayers in the form of tax rebates and reduced tax rates.

The most recent attempts to control deficits occurred in the 2011 fight over raising the debt ceiling. The Budget Control Act of 2011 raised the debt ceiling but required trillions of dollars of deficit reduction from projected budget deficits over the succeeding 10 years.[199] (See Chapter 8 for more about the 2011 debt debates.)

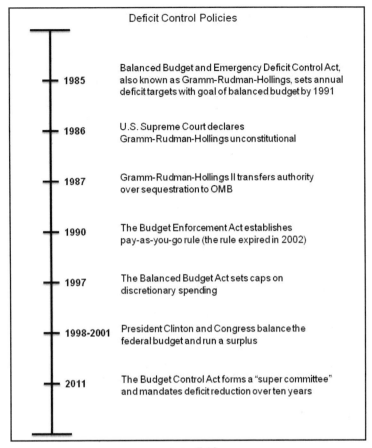

Deficit Control Policies

1985 — Balanced Budget and Emergency Deficit Control Act, also known as Gramm-Rudman-Hollings, sets annual deficit targets with goal of balanced budget by 1991

1986 — U.S. Supreme Court declares Gramm-Rudman-Hollings unconstitutional

1987 — Gramm-Rudman-Hollings II transfers authority over sequestration to OMB

1990 — The Budget Enforcement Act establishes pay-as-you-go rule (the rule expired in 2002)

1997 — The Balanced Budget Act sets caps on discretionary spending

1998-2001 — President Clinton and Congress balance the federal budget and run a surplus

2011 — The Budget Control Act forms a "super committee" and mandates deficit reduction over ten years

FIGURE 7.10

1) Deficits occur when government spending is greater than revenues in a given year.
2) Federal debt is the accumulation of past years' budget deficits. Deficits add to federal debt while surpluses pay down the debt.
3) The use of deficits and the creation of the national debt go back to the early years of the US government. Deficits, not

surpluses, are the norm. In nearly three-fourths of the years since 1900, the government has run deficits.

Balanced Budget is a budget in which government revenues and government spending are equal in a given year.

Debt is money owed. Also see **federal debt.**

Debt Ceiling is the legal limit set by Congress on the total amount that the US Treasury can borrow.

Debt Held by Federal Accounts is the debt that is held by the government itself. It occurs when surpluses in federal government accounts are invested in Treasury securities.

Deficit results when government expenditures are greater than tax collections in a given year. In order to fund a deficit, the Treasury borrows money by selling bonds or other securities.

Federal Debt is the sum of all past federal budget deficits, minus what that the federal government has repaid.

Sequestration is automatic spending cuts.

Surplus is the amount by which revenues exceed expenditures in the federal budget. The federal government has only run a surplus in four years in the last half-century, from 1998 to 2001.

EIGHT

The President's 2013 Budget Request

"Think about the America within our reach...."
—President Barack Obama, State of the Union Address, January 2012

The budget process described in Chapter 4 is how the process is supposed to go, but it doesn't always turn out that way in practice. There is tremendous conflict in Washington and around the country about federal spending—how large spending should be, what the federal government should spend money on, and how much it should be allowed to borrow.

The 2012 elections add to the conflict by raising the stakes for elected officials who hope to be re-elected in November. The elections also raise the stakes for people like you, since polarization in Washington over federal spending and deficits means the candidates who win in 2012 will make crucial decisions about spending priorities in the next few years. Before going into the details of President Obama's 2013 budget request, this chapter gives you some important background on budget politics in Washington.

A Couple Bumpy Years for the Federal Budget

On October 1, 2010, fiscal year 2011 began with *none* of the usual 12 appropriations bills enacted. Instead, lawmakers used continuing resolutions to fund the government. A continuing resolution is a piece of legislation that temporarily extends funding for federal agencies, usually at the same levels appropriated in the previous year. Congress passed eight continuing resolutions before it passed a 2011 budget, six months into the fiscal year.

Then, in August 2011, the federal debt hit the debt ceiling. The debt ceiling is the legal limit on how much debt the federal government allows itself to hold. Many lawmakers said they would not vote to raise the debt ceiling, and instead argued that the right thing to do was to make deep cuts in federal spending. Failing to raise the debt ceiling, however, would have prevented the Treasury from making interest payments on the government's accumulated debt, and thus would have forced the US Treasury to default on its loans. So lawmakers ultimately did agree to raise the debt ceiling, and that agreement came in the Budget Control Act of 2011. The Budget Control Act mandated $917 billion in cuts to nonmilitary discretionary spending over 10 years, and formed a 12-member committee made up of lawmakers from both parties drawn from both the House and Senate. That group of lawmakers, nicknamed the super committee, was tasked with devising a plan for at least $1.2 trillion in additional deficit reduction over the coming decade.

But the super committee did not come up with a plan for $1.2 trillion in deficit reduction. According to the Budget Control Act, its failure to do so triggers $1.2 trillion in sequestration, or automatic spending cuts, to begin in January 2013. Many lawmakers, however, hope to come up with a plan to avoid sequestration, since it would bring deep across-the-board cuts to domestic programs as well as to the military.

What *Is* the President's Budget Request?

As Chapter 4 explains, the president is required by law to submit a budget proposal, also called a budget request, to Congress every February. But given the recent track record of Congress—with lawmakers frequently using continuing resolutions to avoid many of their usual budgeting responsibilities—and because it's an election year, many Washington insiders don't expect Congress to pass any budget at all in 2012. Instead, many people expect that lawmakers will ignore the president's budget and instead will use continuing resolutions to fund the government through the November elections.

It was in this climate that President Obama released his budget for fiscal year 2013. Given that the actual federal budget in 2013 likely won't look much like the president's request, does his budget matter?

There are several reasons why the president's budget is still important. First, the budget is the president's vision for the country in 2013 and beyond, and it reflects input from every federal agency about which programs are important and deserve sustained or expanded funding, and which programs can be trimmed or eliminated. In an election year and at a time of conflict over federal spending, the president's budget is in large part a political document, but an important one because it lays out his priorities in great detail.

The budget is also important because it provides a blueprint for how the spending cuts of the Budget Control Act should be distributed among different kinds of federal programs. And it offers a plan for what should be done about the Bush tax cuts, which have been law for a decade and have cost the US Treasury trillions of dollars in revenue. Finally, the budget is important because it serves as a benchmark against which all subsequent spending legislation will be measured.

The New Budget

President Obama proposed $3.67 trillion in new budget authority in his 2013 request. His budget begins to phase in the $917 billion of cuts imposed by the Budget Control Act, but proposes avoiding sequestration by achieving the required deficit reduction in other ways, mostly by raising taxes on wealthy Americans. A February 2012 poll found that 85 percent of Americans favored raising taxes on the wealthy to help reduce budget deficits.[200] Tax rates are an area of particular conflict between President Obama and Republican lawmakers in Congress, many of whom have stated their opposition to tax increases of any kind. So the president's proposal to reduce deficits by raising taxes on the wealthy may indeed remain as nothing more than a proposal.

Figure 8.1 shows the federal budget over two decades, including projections through 2017. The spike in 2009 is the result of stimulus spending in response to the Great Recession, and the downward trend after 2012 reflects the cuts of the Budget Control Act. While the president projects federal spending to begin increasing again after 2014, that increase is due entirely to growth in mandatory spending, which is largely unaffected by the Budget Control Act.

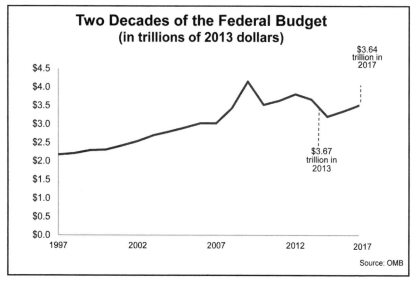

FIGURE 8.1

You can see the entirety of the president's new budget divided into different kinds of spending in Figure 8.2. As compared to federal spending in 2011, which is illustrated in Chapter 6 in Figure 6.2, you can see that Social Security, Unemployment & Labor takes up a slightly larger share of the budget in 2013, and the same goes for Medicare & Health. Military spending takes up a slightly smaller share, coming in at 18 percent.

Discretionary Spending Declines, Mandatory Grows as Shares of the Budget

The president proposed a discretionary budget of $1.15 trillion in 2013. As compared to 2012 levels, nonmilitary discretionary spending—which includes education spending, as well as most domestic programs, and funding for science, energy, and the environment—declined by 5 percent. Military spending, including funding for wars in Iraq and Afghanistan, declined by 6 percent, though the Department of Defense base budget—which excludes war operations—declined by 2.6 percent. These reductions reflect caps on discretionary spending mandated in the Budget Control Act. See "Military Spending in 2013 and Beyond" for more about funding for the Department of Defense and war costs.

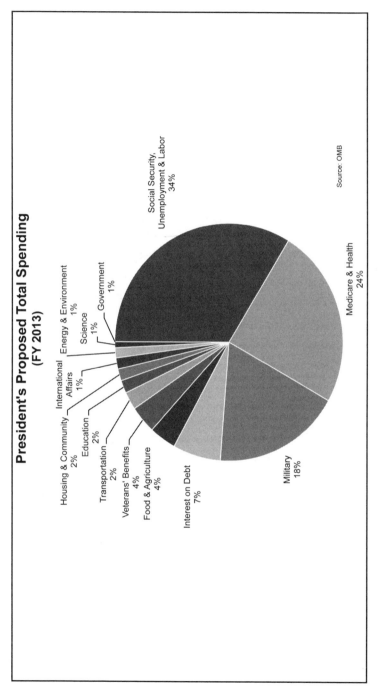

President's Proposed Total Spending (FY 2013)

Social Security, Unemployment & Labor 34%

Medicare & Health 24%

Military 18%

Interest on Debt 7%

Food & Agriculture 4%

Veterans' Benefits 4%

Transportation 2%

Education 2%

Housing & Community 2%

International Affairs 1%

Energy & Environment 1%

Science 1%

Government 1%

Source: OMB

FIGURE 8.2

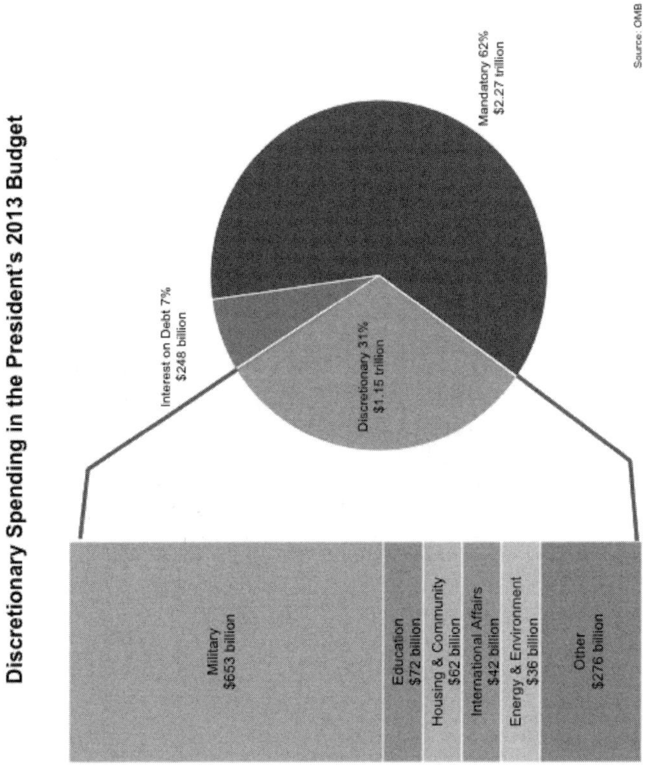

Discretionary Spending in the President's 2013 Budget

Interest on Debt 7%
$248 billion

Mandatory 62%
$2.27 trillion

Discretionary 31%
$1.15 trillion

Military
$653 billion

Education
$72 billion

Housing & Community
$62 billion

International Affairs
$42 billion

Energy & Environment
$36 billion

Other
$276 billion

Source: OMB

FIGURE 8.3

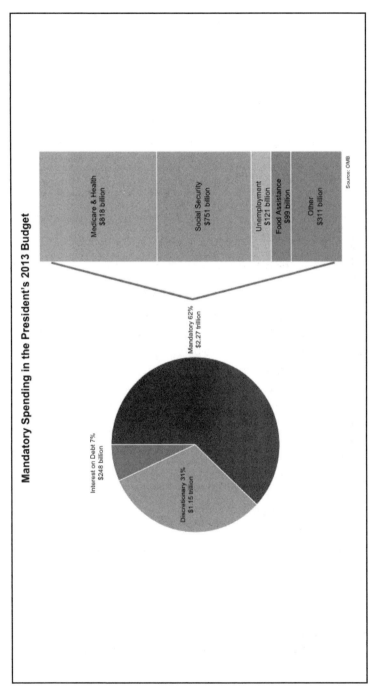

FIGURE 8.4

Figure 8.3 shows how the new budget is divided into mandatory and discretionary spending and interest on debt and then details where the $1.15 trillion in discretionary spending would go. Mandatory spending is growing as a share of the overall budget, projected at $2.27 trillion in 2013, or 62 percent of all federal spending. The majority of that money funds the Social Security and Medicare programs, which are overwhelmingly popular with the American public. A September 2011 poll found that more than 70 percent of Americans oppose cuts to those programs, with fully 77 percent of Americans opposing cuts to Social Security.[201] Figure 8.4 shows how the $2.27 trillion in mandatory spending breaks down between those programs and other kinds of mandatory spending.

Where the Money Comes From in 2013

A plan for federal spending is really only half of the president's budget. The other half is revenues: How much money does the president expect to raise from taxes in 2013, and from what sources? The budget projects total tax revenue in fiscal 2013 to be $2.9 trillion, which is about 16 percent greater than in 2012. Figure 8.5 shows where the president expects that money to come from.

As compared to recent years, payroll taxes make up a smaller share of total revenues—33 percent in 2013, down from 36 percent in 2011 and 34 percent in 2012. The president and Congress have temporarily reduced the payroll-tax rate. Normally workers pay 6.2 percent of their wages to fund Social Security, but through Dec. 31, 2012, they'll pay just 4.2 percent. That lower rate reduces overall tax revenues, and, since these taxes fund Social Security, the payroll-tax holiday reduces the dedicated funding source for that program.

It's the Economy

Recall from Chapter 4 that the president's budget makes numerous assumptions about the economy in order to estimate safety-net spending and tax revenues in the coming year. In order for the federal government to raise the projected $2.9 trillion in revenues in 2013, those assumptions must prove to be more or less accurate.

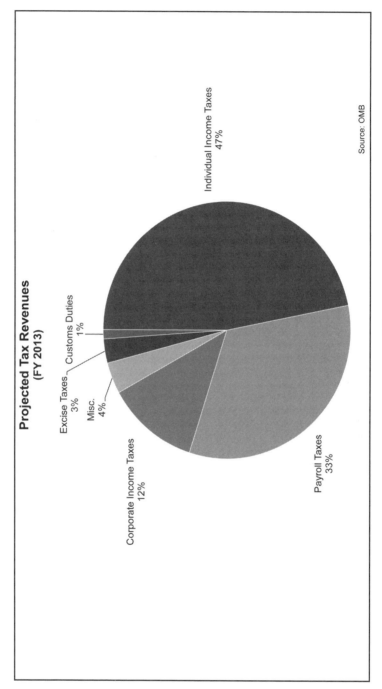

Projected Tax Revenues
(FY 2013)

Individual Income Taxes
47%

Payroll Taxes
33%

Corporate Income Taxes
12%

Misc.
4%

Excise Taxes
3%

Customs Duties
1%

Source: OMB

FIGURE 8.5

When You Assume...

In addition to guiding the allocation of federal resources, the economic assumptions in the annual budget request can be used to support a particular policy or political agenda. For example, according to President Obama's 2013 budget, "certain tax reductions enacted in 2001 and 2003 are assumed to be permanent for purposes of calculating revenue estimates."[202] Those "tax reductions" are the Bush-era tax cuts, which have cost the US Treasury trillions of dollars since 2001 and which are currently scheduled to expire on Dec. 31, 2012. President Obama's budget, however, assumes that all of those tax cuts will become permanent, even though there is no action in Congress to suggest that will be the case.

But that's not all. Once the president's budget makes this speculative assumption, it then proposes eliminating the tax cuts for wealthy people—individuals making over $200,000 a year or families making over $250,000. Why would the budget first assume the tax cuts to be permanent, then later in the same document propose letting the tax cuts expire for only some Americans?

Because once it has assumed all the tax cuts will be permanent, letting some of the tax cuts expire appears to raise substantial additional revenues, which the president then highlights as part of his deficit reduction plan.

That's an accounting trick. Under current law, tax revenues would be far higher than they would be if all of the provisions of the president's budget were enacted, because all of the Bush tax cuts would expire.

Not surprisingly, though, given the complexity of the economy, the president's assumptions are often incorrect. The economic assumptions in the 2012 budget were too optimistic; the economic recovery has been slower than OMB planned. But in the 2013 budget the projections have been too *pessimistic*. The president's new budget projected an unemployment rate of 8.9 percent for fiscal year 2012, 8.6 percent in 2013, and 8.1 percent in 2014.[203] But the unemployment rate was already well below 8.9 percent as of February 2012, hovering around 8.3 percent. The new budget also assumed annual GDP growth of 2.7 percent in fiscal 2012, and actual growth is now likely to exceed that estimate.

The Deficit

If the president is correct about spending levels as well as tax revenues in 2013—that is, if the Treasury indeed collects $2.9 trillion in taxes—then the federal government will run a deficit of roughly $901 billion in the 2013 fiscal year. That's down from $1.3 trillion in fiscal 2012, a reduction of more than 30 percent. Figure 8.6 illustrates the share of total revenues in 2013 that will come from borrowing.

The new budget projects further decreases in the deficit over each of the next five years, with the budget deficit dropping to $612 billion, or 3 percent of GDP, by fiscal 2017.[204, 205] That's down from a high of 10 percent of GDP in 2009, during the height of the Great Recession.

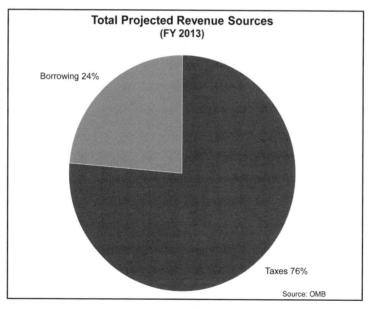

FIGURE 8.6

In all, the Obama administration estimates that the new budget request will result in $4 trillion in deficit reduction over 10 years, as compared to previous projections. (See "When You Assume…" above for an inside peak at how the president calculates that $4 trillion.) In addition to reducing spending, the budget achieves $4 trillion in deficit reduction from the increased tax revenues that result from the stronger economy; reductions in war spending in Iraq and Afghanistan; and changes in the tax code that raise taxes on wealthy Americans and close some corporate tax loopholes.

Because of the super committee's failure to recommend $1.2 trillion in deficit reduction for the next 10 years, the Budget Control Act mandates that sequestration will take effect in January 2013. Sequestration would result in across-the-board cuts to discretionary spending amounting to more than $100 billion each year. As noted above, however, the president's budget does not project that sequestration will occur, and therefore it does not account for its impact on spending or deficits in the coming years.

Health Care Spending Continues to Grow

President Obama's new budget estimates that spending on health care programs will cost the federal government $897 billion in fiscal year 2013; $530 billion of that will go to Medicare. Health spending is the fastest growing kind of federal spending, comprising 24 percent of the president's 2013 request. Less than four decades ago, federal spending for health care was only 7 percent of the budget.

There are many reasons health care costs are rising, and there are also numerous myths about those rising costs. One myth is that the cost of Medicare is rising faster than the cost of all other kinds of health care in this country. In fact, *all* health care costs are rising, and Medicare spending is rising at a slightly *slower* rate than spending on private health care.[206] Furthermore, rising health care costs are not unique to the United States. Health care in other industrialized nations is getting more expensive too,[207] though the US spends more on health care than its peer nations do.[208]

So what's behind the steep increases in the cost of health care? While there are numerous factors that contribute to grow-

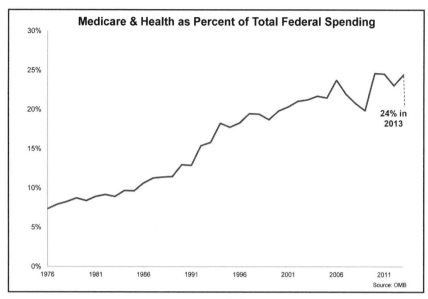

FIGURE 8.7

ing health care costs, such as demographic changes, the biggest driver of rising costs is technology, according to the Congressional Budget Office and numerous health care economists. A century ago, health care was very inexpensive because there was little that doctors knew how to do, so there wasn't much to pay for. But technological advances have given doctors ways to treat just about everything, and health care has gotten more and more expensive as a result.

Lawmakers in Washington are searching for ways to control health spending, and President Obama's 2010 health care reform legislation, the Patient Protection and Affordable Care Act, sought to impose some mechanisms that would contain costs. That's a tricky task, since lawmakers face overwhelming public support for federal health care programs and overwhelming opposition to any changes or cuts. A January 2011 poll found that only 8 percent of Americans would support major reductions to Medicare, while 56 percent said there should be no cuts at all to the program.

Health care economists and other experts are developing ways to help the federal government control health costs. For example, the US Department of Health and Human Services recently announced that it would begin something called "bundled payments" in the Medicare program.[209] That means that the federal government will pay a single fee to some health care providers for patients' whole health "episodes"—such as heart bypass—rather than paying for each test, procedure, and medicine administered. That's intended to give health professionals an incentive to improve coordination of care and to reduce duplicative or unnecessary procedures.

One reason the Medicare program is so popular is that it has been highly successful at bringing health care with relatively low out-of-pocket costs to nearly every senior citizen in the United States. Medicaid, the health care program for low-income Americans that is jointly funded by the federal government and the 50 states, also enjoys wide popularity. In a January 2011 poll, 86 percent of Americans opposed major cuts to Medicaid. And while Medicare has successfully reached nearly every American senior, Medicaid has not done the same for low-income families. According to the Census Bureau, 8.5 percent of all children in the United States and 17 percent of all adults have no health insurance.[210] It would cost an estimated additional $190 billion per year to provide health insurance for all of them, based on the costs of the Medicaid program.[211] The 2010 health care reform legislation attempts to dramatically increase the number of Americans who have health insurance. The federal government, the states, employers, and individuals would all share in the cost.

Military Spending in 2013 and Beyond

President Obama's new budget includes $525 billion for the Department of Defense (DoD, also called the Pentagon). Adjusted for inflation, that's 2.6 percent less than fiscal 2012 levels. The American public is divided about whether the federal government should reduce military spending. For example, in a recent poll, 45 percent said a smaller military can be just as effective, while 44 percent said cuts will reduce effectiveness.[212] The 2.6 percent decline is the first cut to the Pentagon's base budget in over a decade.

The $525 billion for the DoD does not include war costs, the US nuclear weapons program, or international military assistance. The president's budget includes $89 billion for military operations in Iraq and Afghanistan. Due to the end of combat operations in Iraq and projected reductions in the number of troops deployed in Afghanistan, that amount represents a 23 percent decline from 2012.

The new budget also includes $17.7 billion for the defense activities at the Department of Energy, a 5.5 percent *increase* relative to current levels. Most of that money funds the nuclear weapons program. And President Obama includes $14 billion in the budget for international military assistance. That represents a roughly constant funding level as compared to 2012. International military assistance funds weapons and training for foreign militaries as well as other kinds of military assistance.

The Pentagon plans to reduce spending by a total of $259 billion over five years and $487 billion over 10 years relative to projections made a year ago in the 2012 budget. To do so, it has proposed reducing the overall number of men and women in uniform over the next five years in both active units and the National Guard and Reserve. Most of the reductions would be in the active Army (13 percent) and Marine Corps (10 percent). Both services would still be larger, however, than they were before the wars in Iraq and Afghanistan began. DoD will also delay or reduce several major weapons programs, and the new budget calls for two new rounds of military base closures in 2013 and 2015.[213]

One cost savings proposal is particularly controversial—changes to the military's health insurance program. Among other provisions, DoD is proposing increases in how much service members would pay in premiums and copayments. The proposed changes would not have a significant impact on current members of the military, retirees, or survivors. According to former Defense Secretary Robert Gates, the Pentagon's health care costs have grown over the decade from $19 billion annually to $50 billion, with no increase in premiums since the TRICARE program began.[214] Many members of Congress, however, are unwilling to consider such increases in costs for service members and their families.

did you know

How Many Miles is the Pentagon Budget?

If you converted $525.4 billion (the proposed Pentagon budget for fiscal 2013) into $1 bills, and laid each bill end to end, it would reach 51.4 million miles. That's enough to go around Earth 2,065 times.

While there is a decline in the DoD base budget in 2013 relative to 2012, the president projects that Pentagon spending will grow in the coming years. Figure 8.8 shows DoD funding projections that were included in the 2012 budget as compared to projections in the 2013 budget. The new projections are lower than the old ones, but Figure 8.8 also shows that from 2013 to 2017 annual Pentagon spending is projected to rise.

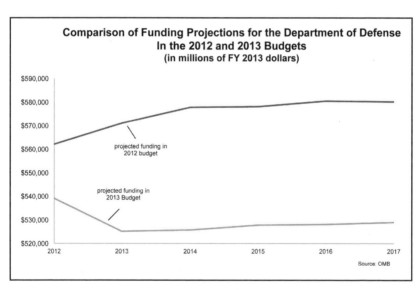

FIGURE 8.8

Funding Education

Education funding in the president's discretionary budget is around $1.5 billion greater than 2012 levels—that's roughly a 2 percent increase. Education is one of the few areas in which the budget calls for an increase over fiscal 2012 levels. Despite widespread public concern about the deficit, a February 2011 poll found that 62 percent of Americans supported more funding for education in the federal budget.[215]

An education initiative in the new budget that has gotten a great deal of attention is an $8 billion multiyear pledge to create a Community College to Career Fund to support training programs that prepare students for high-skilled jobs. The program would be administered jointly between the Department of Education and the Department of Labor, and would create new partnerships between community colleges and businesses to train and place 2 million workers in high-growth industries.[216]

Despite this new initiative and the overall increase in education funding, education has historically accounted for very little of the total federal budget, as you can see in Figure 8.9. And the president's new budget puts education funding at 2 percent of total spending, which is roughly the share of the budget that has

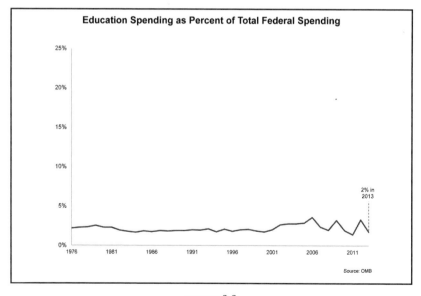

FIGURE 8.9

gone to education since 1976, the earliest year for which comprehensive budget authority data are available.

The increasing cost of a college education is also a major issue, particularly as the continued poor economic climate forces states to reduce their support for public education. As a result, an increasing number of graduates are leaving school with higher levels of debt. The president's new budget seeks to reward schools that contain their costs by providing more than $10 billion in student financial aid grants and loans specifically for students at those schools, and especially for economically disadvantaged students.[217] The new budget also includes $36.7 billion in available aid for the Pell Grant program, which provided need-based grants to 9.6 million college students in 2012. The 2013 funding level is a slight increase over 2012 levels.[218]

1) The president is required by law to submit a budget request every February for the coming fiscal year. Even though the actual federal budget in 2013 likely won't look a lot like the president's request, the president's budget is still important. It's the president's vision for the country in 2013 and beyond and it reflects input from every federal agency. And this year the budget gives a blueprint for how the spending cuts of the Budget Control Act should be distributed among different kinds of federal programs, and a plan for what should be done about the Bush tax cuts, which have been law for a decade and expire at the end of 2012.

2) Because of the cuts of the Budget Control Act, discretionary spending as a share of the total federal budget declines in 2013. Mandatory spending, which is largely exempt from the cuts of the Budget Control Act, takes up a larger share of the

overall budget, and will increase—both in dollar terms and as a percent of the budget—in coming years.

3) In 2013 the president projects a deficit of $901 billion. That's a reduction of more than 30 percent relative to 2012. In part because of cuts in the Budget Control Act, and in part because of policy proposals that include raising some tax rates for wealthy Americans, the deficit is projected to decline to 3 percent of GDP by fiscal 2017, down from its high of 10 percent in 2009.

NINE

Take Action

"If you're not at the table, you're probably on the menu."
—Unknown

Chapter 1 introduced the notion of democracy and how all Americans have a right as well as a responsibility to weigh in on the political process. Chapter 1 also explained that many people are confused by the federal budget, which may keep them from voicing their own priorities for where tax dollars should be spent.

As Representative Barbara Jordan said, "If you're going to play the game properly you'd better know every rule." Now you know the rules. You've made it through *A People's Guide to the Federal Budget*, and you're a budget expert. In Chapter 4 you learned the steps of the annual budget process. In Chapter 6, Figure 6.6 showed you where every penny of your federal income tax dollars went in 2011. Out of every dollar, 27 cents went to Military; 21.4 cents went to Medicare & Health; 2.5 cents went to Education; and 1 cent went to Science.

In Figure 6.2 you saw a breakdown of total federal spending, which includes your income tax dollars as well as all other kinds of tax collections and money the federal government borrows. You saw that 32 percent of all federal spending went to Social Security, Unemployment & Labor in 2011; 20 percent went to Military; and 3 percent went to Housing & Community. In Chapter 5 you read about how the federal government raises the trillions of tax dollars it spends each year. You read about different tax rates for different levels of income; you read about corporate taxes; payroll taxes; and something called the "Buffet rule." In Chapter 7 you read about deficits and federal debt, and how the federal government borrows money and pays interest on the money it borrows. In Chapter 8 you read about how President Obama proposes spending $3.67 trillion in fiscal year 2013.

Now you have the chance to consider whether the federal budget reflects *your* priorities. As some wise person once said, "If you're not at the table, you're probably on the menu." If you don't speak up about where you want your tax dollars spent, others gladly will speak up for you—and you may not like what they have to say. This chapter gives you the tools you need to make yourself heard. All the resources listed in this chapter, as well as new and updated resources, are listed on the National Priorities Project Web site at: http://www.nationalpriorities.org/resources/take-action/.

Know Who Represents You

You are represented in Congress by two senators from your state and one representative from a district within your state. You can find your elected officials' Web sites through a search in the top right-hand corner of:

http://www.house.gov and http://www.senate.gov.

You can also find them through: http://www.opencongress.com.

Open Congress offers information on bills your representatives have sponsored, their voting records, media mentions, and much more.

Register to Vote

Registering to vote is a crucial part of participating in the democratic process. You can't vote in elections without first registering. You can register through http://www.rockthevote.org, or you can register by mail. Download the National Mail Voter Registration form at:

http://www.eac.gov/voter_resources/register_to_vote.aspx.

If you're a college student and are registered at home rather than where you go to school, you can find state-specific assistance on getting absentee ballots at:

http://www.longdistancevoter.org/absentee_ballots.

Once you're registered, pay attention to election dates and to the voting location for your precinct so you're in the right place

at the right time to cast your vote. A good resource to keep on top of election dates and polling locations is:
http://www.vote411.org.

Stay Informed

Voting is important, but it's also important to be well informed about the issues and candidates when you enter the voting booth. Stay up to date with activity in Washington and in your local community.

- Read the newspaper. *The Washington Post* and *The New York Times* have good coverage of what's going on in Washington.
- Check news Web sites. The Capitol Hill newspaper *The Hill* is a good resource for action in Congress and the White House. Visit its Web site at http://www.thehill.com.
- Follow news organizations on Facebook and Twitter.
- Listen to news on the radio.
- Talk to other people about current events.
- Sign up for Google News email alerts, for example for the term "federal budget" or for the names of your senators and representative.

You can find more detailed suggestions about how to stay informed by visiting:
http://www.nationalpriorities.org/resources/take-action/.

Contact Your Representatives

There are a variety of ways to express your views about budget priorities, ranging in ease from sending a tweet to visiting Washington for a face-to-face meeting with a legislator. Remember, while you are free to contact any member of Congress, you will be most effective by contacting legislators who represent you directly.

Phone Calls

Calling your senator or representative is much less scary than it sounds and usually takes less than a minute of your time. You can find phone numbers on their Web sites, or call the US Capitol Switchboard at 202-224-3121 and ask to be transferred. One way

Timing Is Everything

Figure 9.1 revisits the annual budget process described in Chapter 4, and then highlights opportunities for you to contact federal officials and lawmakers to voice your budget priorities. You are most likely to be successful at influencing the federal budget by targeting your efforts to the appropriate stages within the process. Thus, Figure 9.1 points out key opportunities to shape the outcome and what issues to discuss when.

The part of the federal budget process that is conducted by the executive branch—which includes the White House and federal agencies—is by nature difficult to influence. That's because agency employees, unlike their colleagues in Congress, generally are not in contact with the public. This portion of the process does not include public hearings or debates. Therefore you will be most effective at influencing the budget during this stage after you have cultivated relationships with officials at the federal agencies that are of significance to you. Agency officials tend to develop relationships with constituents and stakeholders who are closely associated with a particular issue. For example, the Department of Energy (DOE), which has jurisdiction over our nation's nuclear weapons complex, has an ongoing relationship with many residents of communities that surround DOE's nuclear weapons facilities. These communities have a long-standing commitment to providing input on nuclear waste management, and they interact directly with DOE officials.

to save time and help you make calling Congress a habit is to save the phone numbers for your legislators' offices in your cell phone.

When you call, ask to speak to the **congressional aide** who handles the issue about which you're calling. Congressional aides are support staff for members of Congress. After identifying yourself on the phone, you can say something as simple as "Please tell Senator/Representative (name) that I support/oppose (bill or issue)." While you can state your reason for support or opposition, do not feel like you have to know the material inside out. The aide will simply keep a count of **constituent** calls and their general positions.

Writing a Letter or E-mail

Personal messages from constituents can be a very effective way of communicating with your legislators. Always be sure to include your name and address to make it clear that you live in the relevant district or state. All letters should start with Dear Senator/Representative, and they can be just a few paragraphs about a single issue.

While you can always use information you have found through various sources, you should write your letter in your own words. Include specific information about the bill or program about which you're writing. Details about personal or local impact are very effective. Always be courteous, and be very clear about what action you'd like your legislator to take.

Find your legislator's mailing address on his or her Web site. Due to security concerns, mail delivery to Capitol Hill offices can be slow. If you are writing a letter about a pressing issue or upcoming vote, be sure to leave extra time for delivery. You can also send a letter by e-mail through your legislator's Web site.

Social Media

The newest and easiest method of contacting your representatives is through social media sites like Facebook and Twitter. While phone calls and letters may still carry more weight in the eyes of lawmakers and congressional aides, speaking to your legislators through social media has the advantage of occurring in the public eye. When you comment on your legislator's Facebook page or send a tweet, other constituents can read your message. This may spark a dialogue. It could also help increase awareness about the issue you're raising and build support for your cause.

To find politicians on Facebook, you can either look for a link on their official Web site or simply look them up through the search bar in Facebook. The Web site http://www.tweetcongress.org

maintains a Twitter directory of members of Congress. You can also use the Twitter search bar to find them, though beware that there are many imposter Twitter accounts in which Twitter users pretend to be elected officials.

Through social media sites you can ask questions, respond to legislators' posts or Tweets, encourage them to take action, thank them when they do something you support, and much more.

Meeting With Your Representative

One of the most powerful ways to have your voice heard is to schedule a personal meeting with your senator or representative. Since all senators and representatives also have local offices in their home states, you could schedule a meeting closer to home so don't have to travel to Washington. If you can travel to Washington for a meeting, call your elected official's Capitol Hill office and ask to schedule a time.

When you call to request a meeting, explain what issue you want to discuss. Remember that legislators are busy people and that it may be hard to get an appointment. Sometimes you will have the opportunity to meet with a congressional aide rather than your legislator.

Before the meeting:

- If possible, ask colleagues or friends who share your concerns to attend the meeting with you.
- Thoroughly research the topic you will be discussing, including opposing views. Write down a list of your concerns and explain the action you would like your legislator to take.
- Research your legislator. You should know the committees on which she serves, her positions on various issues, and her recent voting record.
- Review the budget process and federal budget glossary so you're not intimidated by budget jargon.
- Practice. If you're going in a small group, give each person an assignment, so that everyone knows the points they are responsible for making.

During the meeting:

- Thank your legislator for taking the time to speak with

you. Be sure to acknowledge any past action—such as a vote or a public statement—that you support.

- Bring several copies of any information you'll need so there are enough for your legislator as well as congressional aides. Always clearly cite any sources you used to prepare the materials.
- Be sure you're very clear about the actions you want your legislator to take. Try to get specific commitments or a date when you should check back about progress on the issue. Write everything down.
- No matter what the response, don't lose your cool.

After the meeting:

- Send thank-you notes to the legislator and congressional aides.
- Check progress by keeping track of your legislator's voting record. The web site http://www.congressionalaudit.org offers a convenient way to get weekly email updates about your elected officials.

If your legislator follows through on your request, write another thank-you letter. If your legislator does not follow through on something he or she committed to during your meeting, contact the appropriate congressional aide and express your disappointment.

Remember that representatives in the House run for re-election every two years, and senators every six years. If you are disappointed with your legislator, you can show your disapproval by supporting another candidate at election time.

Other Important Ways to Stay Politically Active

- Write a letter to the editor.
- Start a petition using resources at http://www.change.org.
- Create your own federal budget and send it to Congress at http://www.buildabetterbudget.org.
- Send your friends and family an e-mail or text message to remind them about Election Day and important issues and elections on the ballot.
- Use government transparency tools and smartphone

apps and share them with others. Find a list of these resources at:

http://www.nationalpriorities.org/en/take-action/transparency-movers-and-shakers/.

- Attend a protest or rally for a cause that's important to you.
- Join or start a political organization in your community using resources from http://www.meetup.com.
- Call in to a radio talk show.
- Start your own radio show on a community or college radio station.
- Run for office and encourage others to do the same.
- Talk to your friends and family about how the federal budget works and how it affects them.

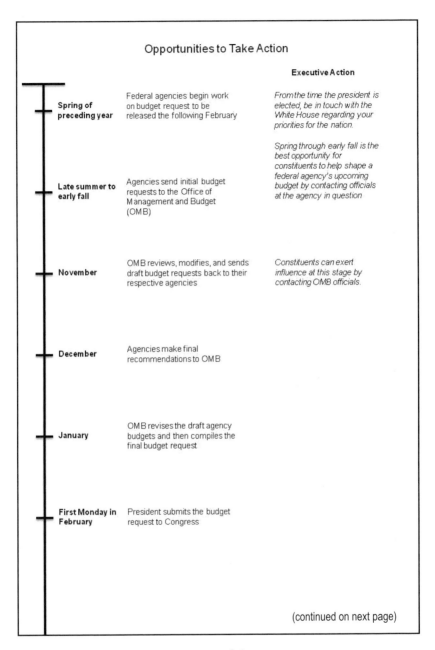

FIGURE 9.1

(continued from previous page)

Opportunities to Take Action

Congressional Action

February to March

Administration and agency officials testify before Congress in support of the budget request

House and Senate Appropriations subcommittees hold hearings with heads of agencies and outside public witnesses

This is a good time to contact lawmakers if you believe the president's budget is wrongly cutting a program, or to voice support for provisions in the budget. Subcommittee members determine who testifies about requested agency funding, and they may ask stakeholders for suggestions on issues they should raise at hearings. You may be able to influence a hearing, or even testify, if you are deeply affected by a particular program.

April

House and Senate Budget Committees draft and vote on budget resolutions to recommend overall funding levels for each federal agency

April and May are good opportunities to speak with lawmakers. First contact members of Budget Committees about agencies' overall spending levels.

Once the budget resolution has passed, constituents should direct their attention to Appropriations subcommittees as they begin to consider funding for specific programs.

The full House and Senate adopt budget resolutions based on recommendations from their respective Budget Committees and then reconcile their separate versions into a single budget resolution

May

Based on the final budget resolution, House and Senate Appropriations Committees set overall funding levels for each of their subcommittees

House Appropriations subcommittees prepare appropriations bills providing funding for specific federal programs

June

Senate Appropriations subcommittees draft revised versions of the House-passed bills

Full Appropriations committees consider subcommittee spending bills

(continued on next page)

(continued from previous page)

July-August — House and Senate pass respective versions of appropriations bills

Once Appropriations subcommittees approve a draft funding bill for the full committee to consider, you have another good opportunity to contact lawmakers about funding for specific programs.

September — House-Senate conference committees meet to resolve differences and agree on final versions of appropriations bills

LAST CHANCE – As House and Senate appropriators iron out differences between their respective versions of appropriations bills, it is critical that lawmakers hear from constituents about which provisions should prevail. For instance, if you support program X, and one chamber has provided significantly more funding for program X than the other chamber has, you should urge lawmakers to include the higher funding level in the final bill.

President signs or vetoes final bills

REALLY LAST CHANCE – If you believe the final version of a bill is deeply problematic, you can urge the president to veto it. But if the White House has not voiced concerns about the bill, then it's not likely that the president will veto it.

October 1 — New fiscal year begins

For any of the 12 annual appropriations bills not yet enacted by October 1, Congress passes continuing resolutions (CRs) to maintain funding for the agencies without appropriations bills. Once Congress completes its work on the outstanding spending bills, they are signed by the president .

1) The federal budget affects everyone. If you don't speak up then other people will, and they may not share your priorities.

2) Registering to vote—and then showing up on Election Day to cast your ballot—is one of the most important things you can do to make sure your voice is heard.

3) There are lots of convenient ways to stay informed about current events and the federal budget.

4) Contacting your elected officials is not scary and is an important part of a healthy democracy.

Constituent is a person who lives in the area that an elected official represents.

Congressional Aides are support staff for members of Congress. They perform a variety of tasks from administrative duties to keeping track of specific policy issues.

Afterword
by Josh Silver

A People's Guide to the Federal Budget is a bridge. Many Americans express dissatisfaction—or worse—over what's happening in Washington today. But many people also say they can't understand much of what's going on, especially when it comes to where our tax dollars go. This book is a bridge for Americans—from dissatisfaction and confusion to knowledge and action.

From Tea Partiers on the right to Occupiers on the left, there is broad agreement among Americans that the influence of money and corporations in our political system has gone too far. And in January 2010, the U.S. Supreme Court case Citizens United v. Federal Election Commission blasted a hole in the already cracked dam. The result was a tidal wave. Corporations and billionaires can now spend any amount to support or unseat politicians.

The 2010 elections saw a record-breaking $489 million spent by outside groups to influence voters—a 450 percent increase over the 2006 cycle. So-called Super PACs are a new breed of political action committees that can raise and spend unlimited sums of money to directly support or oppose candidates. By March 2012, such independent expenditures had doubled as compared to similar expenditures during the entire 2008 elections—this more than seven months before Election Day.

There is also a well-known revolving door between Capitol Hill and the lobbying industry on K Street in Washington. A recent study showed members of Congress who leave their work as legislators to become lobbyists enjoy an average 1,452 percent raise in pay. Their staffers win similar raises. According to another report, nearly 5,400 former members of Congress and their staffers left Capitol Hill to become lobbyists during the past decade: some 45 per month.

As *A People's Guide* notes, there are 24 registered lobbyists for every member of the House and Senate. And that number would be much higher but for loopholes that allow significant lobbying activity without actually registering. An American University study estimates an additional 90,000 people are unregistered but are also part of DC's special-interest influence machine. With massive resources, they barrage policymakers and exploit wedge issues. It prevents lawmakers and voters from working together to tackle the real problems facing the country.

The rise of special-interest power is particularly dangerous at a time when media outlets are shedding journalists, replacing expensive, critical reporting with polarizing TV and radio opinion shows. The result is a citizenry long on opinions and short on facts, vulnerable to manipulations by ideologues and well-paid spin masters who bend public opinion, elections and policy to their own benefit.

In 2012, the window of political opportunity has swung open in a most unusual way. In a rare moment of unity, grassroots conservatives and liberals wholeheartedly agree that a few billionaires should not be allowed to buy our democracy. Occupiers and Tea Partiers together have drawn our attention to a wave of resentment over corruption and moneyed interests in government. Seventy-five percent of Republicans and 84 percent of Democrats oppose the Citizens United decision. Seventy-seven percent of Americans believe Congress must address campaign finance reform; 69 percent believe that Super PACs should be outlawed.

People of all political stripes are outraged. But as Congresswoman Barbara Jordan said, "If you're going to play the game properly you'd better know every rule." That's what makes *A People's Guide* essential. We've got to understand what's going on in Washington so that we can work together and change the rules, so that our elections are not auctions. We need to build the movement for reform—so that our democracy, and the way our tax dollars are spent, reflects the will of the people, and not the will of a wealthy few. All Americans who hope to make their voices heard in Washington must understand that we must take on the issue of money in politics, and play to win.

Josh Silver is CEO of United Republic, a new, nonpartisan organization challenging the undue influence of well-financed special interests over American politics and government. United Republic seeks to transform our nation's smoldering outrage over corruption, gridlock, and bailouts into a strong political force that can bring lasting structural reforms. Silver is a veteran election and media reform executive. He cofounded and served for nine years as president of Free Press, the nation's leading media and technology reform advocacy organization. He has also served as director of development for the cultural arm of the Smithsonian Institution.

Appendix for Educators

*"Education is not the filling of a pail
but the lighting of a fire."*
—William Butler Yeats (1865-1935),
the first Irishman awarded the Nobel Prize for Literature

A Letter to Educators

"Why can't the government give more money for education?" a student in a US history class asks.

Another student quickly responds, "They'd have to take money from something else like food stamps."

"Who's 'they'?" asks the teacher.

"What do you mean, 'who's they'? Them. The government. Congress. The president. Them," a third student chimes in.

And so a discussion of the federal budget and the role of citizens begins in history classes across the nation. What the educator thought would be a brief introduction to New Deal spending becomes a convoluted maze as she/he attempts to describe the history of the United States federal budget to a class of 29 students.

National Priorities Project created *A People's Guide to the Federal Budget* for precisely these moments—for these students and their teachers who deserve to dive into a text that is more than an academic exercise. Educators draw students into their civics curricula, and in so doing they light a fire, as William Butler Yeats called it. They light fire as students learn about how decisions made in Washington affect their own lives and the lives of everyone around them. Educators help their students through a tangled and highly politicized process to see why it is crucial to understand how lawmakers create the federal budget, and why our democracy will languish without our participation.

A People's Guide to the Federal Budget and National Priorities Project's Web site are resources for educators working to make complex federal budget issues comprehensible. Each chapter of *A People's Guide* stands alone, offering in-depth material on one area within the federal budget. NPP's Web site further expands chapter topics with in-depth publications, blog posts, online tools, and more.

In addition, NPP has created a companion menu of authentic, challenging and fun activities—a teacher toolkit. This toolkit makes the content of *A People's Guide* and the NPP Web site even more accessible for a diverse body of middle school, high school, and college-age learners, as its activities allow for differentiated instruction grounded in the following best practices guiding education in this century:

- Curricula should "engage students in a comprehensive process of confronting multiple dilemmas, and encourage students to speculate, think critically, and make personal and civic decisions based on information from multiple perspectives," as stated by expert Judith Pace.[219]
- Educators should have students use data and multiple sources, evaluate point of view and purpose, integrate knowledge and ideas, develop arguments, research to build and present knowledge, and write often. Teachers are urged to focus on critical thinking and problem solving, communication, collaboration, and creativity and innovation—as well as technology and content.[220]

Together, *A People's Guide to the Federal Budget*, the NPP Web site, and the companion Educator Toolkit are components of a vibrant program for developing civic participation and efficacy.

A People's Guide Educator Toolkit can be found at http://www.nationalpriorities.org/en/budget-basics/educator-toolkit/. Some activities in the toolkit use the guide as the primary resource, while others invite the educator and students to access portions of NPP's Web site or an associated online tool. Some activities are comparatively short, serving as activators. Others incorporate several extensions.

Each activity will help students see the connections between their own community and federal spending and revenue policies—for example, how decisions made in the federal budget process affect the resources in high school classrooms, as well as the financial aid available to assist students' enrollment in college. These activities require students to learn and use new vocabulary, as well as to analyze data, synthesize and integrate information from multiple disciplines, and forge strong connections between what they are learning and their life experience.

Through these activities, students will be able to examine discrete components of the federal budget, such as the magnitude of federal spending in their own town and tax dollars generated from their state. Students will be able to use technology, read various perspectives, and draw their own informed and data-driven conclusions. Educators can use a few chapters from *A People's Guide* or the entire book in their efforts to integrate federal budget material into history, mathematics, civics, English Language Arts, or economics curricula. The rich array of resources can also be incorporated into advisories or Community Service graduation requirements.

Educators are invited to tell National Priorities Project how they've used *A People's Guide* in their classrooms, and then NPP will use its Web site as a central place to compile lessons and activities from educators across the country to create a shared resource for all. What's more, the federal budget experts at National Priorities Project have committed to talk with any educator who has questions about the material in this book. They invite you to call 413-584-9556 with your questions.

Join us in using and expanding the Educator Toolkit found at http://www.nationalpriorities.org/en/budget-basics/educator-toolkit. See a small sample of activities below. Our thanks to Jason Auclair, Julliette Burque, Jake Hulseberg, and Adam Tanguay for joining us in this effort.

With all best wishes for your work in the classroom!

Donna Harlan & Ann Hennessey

Dr. Donna Harlan has been a public school educator since 1969, in Texas, Vermont and Massachusetts, serving as a teacher in grades PK–12, professor of education in higher education institutions, building-based principal, and superintendent of schools.

Ms. Ann Hennessey has been an educator in public school and special education settings for 18 years. She has taught international baccalaureate and advanced placement courses and is currently social studies supervisor at Chicopee High School in Chicopee, Massachusetts.

Two Sample Activators for High School Learners

First Activator
Title: Four Corners

Objective: Students will be able to articulate a position (verbally and in writing) on an element of the federal budget.

Description: A Four Corners activity is generally used as a discussion starter. It also may be used as the focal point of an entire lesson. Print the four following statements and post one in each corner of the classroom:

- Strongly Agree
- Simply Agree
- Strongly Disagree
- Simply Disagree

The teacher or a student leader will read a posted statement to the class. After the statement is read, all students will move to one of the four corners of the room based on their reaction and opinion. No one may stand in the middle; everyone must take a position. Students should be given no more than 30 seconds to make their decision.

Once all students are in a corner, the teacher or student leader asks students (some or all) why they chose their position. Only one student at a time may speak. After everyone speaks, the teacher or student leader asks if anyone wants to change position. Discussion follows if students change corners.

Sample Statements: The following sample statements for use in Four Corners pertain to Chapter 6: Where Does the Money Go?

- Statement: The federal government should increase foreign aid.
- Statement: The federal government should increase military spending.
- Statement: The federal government should eliminate food stamps.
- Statement: Earmarks should be eliminated.

Second Activator

Title: Write and Respond

Objective: Students will be able to express their ideas, feelings, and questions about democracy in writing and verbally.

Description: Write and Respond is a prereading activity and is generally used to introduce a lesson or unit by focusing the class on one concept or idea. The teacher posts a statement at the front of the classroom and students write about what the statement means to them, what it makes them think about, and what questions they have about it, for five minutes. Afterward, students find a partner and share for two minutes each what they wrote during the exercise.

Sample Prompt: The following sample prompt pertains to Chapter 1: Why You Should Care about the Federal Budget.

- Quotation by Barbara Jordan: "Democracy is not a spectator sport."

Two Sample Chapter Activities

First Chapter Activity

Title: Small Group Post-Chapter Discussion

Objective: Students will be able to discuss the impact of government decisions on their lives.

Description: Students are assigned to groups of three or four members consisting of Leader, Recorder, Reporter, and Time-keeper. Students will discuss questions on a specific topic and report back to class.

The leader keeps the group on task and ensures everyone has an opportunity to speak. The recorder takes notes about the discussion. The reporter offers a summary to the class and teacher. The timekeeper keeps track of time to make sure the group finishes within the allotted time slot.

Sample Questions for Group Discussion: These sample questions pertain to Chapter 1: Why You Should Care about the Federal Budget.

- What does your group believe the federal government funds within your local community?
- What information did the polling numbers provide?
- In your group's opinion, why is there such a large gap between the percentage of people who said they used a government program versus those who actually did?
- What kinds of spending would you cut in the federal budget? Why?
- Is there anything that you would never cut? Why?
- Chapter 1 states that you can make a difference. Brainstorm specific ways that you can make a difference.

Second Chapter Activity

Title: Whole Class Pre-Chapter Activity for Chapter 5: Where Does the Money Come From?

Objective: Students will be able to articulate how tax dollars are allocated among different spending categories.

Description: Teacher facilitates an all-class activity primarily focused on individual federal income taxes.

On a very large piece of paper or multiple pieces of paper taped together, the teacher draws 13 vertical bars of equal height. Label the bars to coincide with NPP's federal spending categories: Social Security, Unemployment & Labor; Medicare & Health; Military; Interest on Debt; Food & Agriculture; Veterans' Benefits; Transportation; Education; Energy & Environment; Housing & Community; International Affairs; Government; and Science. As students enter the classroom, hand each one 10 circular stickers or sticky notes. Once assembled, invite the students to pretend that they have just paid one dollar in federal income taxes. Tell the students that their ten stickers are worth ten cents each, and explain that each of the ten stickers symbolizes 10 percent of a tax dollar.

Briefly describe the bar chart you have created and explain the definition of each spending category. It is *very* important that students understand each spending category.

Invite students to gather around the bar chart and place their stickers on the empty bars to correspond with where they want the federal government to spend their one federal income tax dollar. Students may spend their tax dollar in any way they choose. For example, if a student thinks the Education category deserves 30 percent of her taxes, she should place three stickers on the Education bar.

Once all students have completed this exercise ask them to take their seats.

Ask for students to volunteer to tell the class where they spent their tax dollar. Ask them why they prioritized their spending the way they did. Allow ample time for students to respond to each other. Encourage students to ask follow-up questions about why their peers chose to spend their tax dollars in the ways they did.

Following this discussion, ask students to write individually for three to five minutes in response to the following questions:

- To which spending category did you give the most stickers? Why?
- To which spending category did you give the fewest stickers? Why?
- Was it difficult to decide how to spend your tax dollar? Why or why not?

At the conclusion of this writing exercise, distribute Figure 6.6: Where Your 2011 Income Tax Dollar Went.

Engage the students with the following questions:

- Do your own priorities match our government's current spending priorities? How are they similar or different?
- What do you think of our government's priorities?

- Would members of this class be able to agree on how their taxes are spent?
- Do you think Congress has a difficult time agreeing on how to spend the trillions of dollars these stickers represent? Why or why not?

Appendix
Federal Spending in the States

Each year, as part of the president's budget request, OMB breaks out expenditures on grant programs to states. This is a reminder of the impact of federal spending on state budgets and the lives of individuals, who receive assistance through state programs that are funded by grants from the federal government.

Figures are in thousands of 2013 dollars.

CHILDREN'S HEALTH INSURANCE PROGRAM
(IN THOUSANDS OF 2013 DOLLARS)

STATE	FY2011	FY2012	FY2013	CHANGE FROM '12 TO '13
AL	$140,236	$143,701	$179,349	+ 24.8 %
AK	$20,531	$21,353	$23,415	+ 9.7 %
AZ	$63,635	$65,706	$27,544	- 58.1 %
AR	$94,065	$96,945	$105,785	+ 9.1 %
CA	$1,299,256	$1,336,047	$1,564,899	+ 17.1 %
CO	$127,865	$132,582	$136,071	+ 2.6 %
CT	$32,427	$33,228	$46,374	+ 39.6 %
DE	$14,050	$14,397	$15,457	+ 7.4 %
DC	$12,413	$12,820	$11,679	- 8.9 %
FL	$336,355	$345,445	$368,755	+ 6.7 %
GA	$247,831	$255,033	$368,964	+ 44.7 %
HI	$34,433	$35,380	$31,073	- 12.2 %
ID	$37,486	$38,574	$43,198	+ 12.0 %
IL	$282,869	$289,859	$295,219	+ 1.8 %
IN	$97,881	$100,300	$132,501	+ 32.1 %
IA	$78,166	$110,801	$99,900	- 9.8 %
KS	$57,839	$59,745	$59,230	- 0.9 %
KY	$134,182	$137,720	$153,662	+ 11.6 %
LA	$192,595	$198,426	$154,928	- 21.9 %
ME	$36,745	$37,652	$31,984	- 15.1 %
MD	$174,744	$179,211	$179,639	+ 0.2 %
MA	$328,159	$336,268	$340,147	+ 1.2 %
MI	$125,246	$128,341	$83,245	- 35.1 %
MN	$21,223	$21,747	$32,308	+ 48.6 %
MS	$166,328	$170,437	$182,126	+ 6.9 %
MO	$116,695	$119,579	$124,000	+ 3.7 %
MT	$39,826	$40,809	$60,762	+ 48.9 %
NE	$40,320	$41,640	$43,392	+ 4.2 %

NV	$24,929	$25,546	$30,487	+ 19.3 %
NH	$13,274	$13,602	$20,379	+ 49.8 %
NJ	$613,122	$628,271	$684,928	+ 9.0 %
NM	$254,170	$262,943	$160,931	- 38.8 %
NY	$544,424	$557,876	$555,731	- 0.4 %
NC	$395,852	$407,880	$390,609	- 4.2 %
ND	$15,797	$16,330	$18,316	+ 12.2 %
OH	$287,791	$294,902	$314,480	+ 6.6 %
OK	$124,645	$128,973	$196,493	+ 52.4 %
OR	$94,322	$96,936	$153,783	+ 58.6 %
PA	$333,224	$341,458	$318,371	- 6.8 %
RI	$31,418	$32,194	$29,929	- 7.0 %
SC	$101,492	$104,166	$101,820	- 2.3 %
SD	$20,776	$21,469	$22,099	+ 2.9 %
TN	$138,970	$142,457	$217,430	+ 52.6 %
TX	$862,150	$897,209	$967,796	+ 7.9 %
UT	$66,175	$68,944	$66,846	- 3.0 %
VT	$5,999	$6,147	$19,215	+ 212.6 %
VA	$181,429	$187,054	$185,589	- 0.8 %
WA	$46,970	$48,409	$80,704	+ 66.7 %
WV	$42,727	$43,783	$48,630	+ 11.1 %
WI	$106,365	$108,992	$93,949	- 13.8 %
WY	$10,342	$10,616	$10,880	+ 2.5 %

COMMUNITY DEVELOPMENT BLOCK GRANT
(IN THOUSANDS OF 2013 DOLLARS)

STATE	FY2011	FY2012	FY2013	CHANGE FROM '12 TO '13
AL	$48,021	$43,197	$39,571	- 8.4 %
AK	$4,494	$3,939	$3,854	- 2.2 %
AZ	$41,675	$53,978	$43,803	- 18.9 %
AR	$25,904	$22,702	$22,214	- 2.2 %
CA	$435,641	$478,928	$368,795	- 23.0 %
CO	$27,824	$40,507	$30,232	- 25.4 %
CT	$39,567	$39,739	$33,622	- 15.4 %
DE	$6,719	$3,871	$3,788	- 2.1 %
DC	$20,330	$31,425	$14,507	- 53.8 %
FL	$205,545	$226,802	$127,878	- 43.6 %
GA	$79,004	$70,705	$66,029	- 6.6 %
HI	$14,136	$12,392	$12,125	- 2.2 %
ID	$12,007	$12,313	$9,918	- 19.4 %
IL	$185,939	$169,899	$139,017	- 18.2 %
IN	$89,985	$59,024	$55,893	- 5.3 %
IA	$133,874	$33,696	$32,971	- 2.2 %
KS	$26,679	$25,276	$22,487	- 11.0 %

KY	$56,824	$37,553	$36,745	- 2.2 %
LA	$369,908	$200,658	$150,736	- 24.9 %
ME	$18,094	$17,786	$15,883	- 10.7 %
MD	$67,518	$58,089	$43,873	- 24.5 %
MA	$106,483	$95,282	$87,192	- 8.5 %
MI	$123,215	$156,164	$105,116	- 32.7 %
MN	$53,188	$47,624	$46,084	- 3.2 %
MS	$39,207	$31,836	$28,479	- 10.5 %
MO	$67,913	$54,891	$53,505	- 2.5 %
MT	$8,619	$7,553	$7,391	- 2.1 %
NE	$17,805	$15,604	$15,269	- 2.1 %
NV	$4,708	$30,705	$16,307	- 46.9 %
NH	$11,786	$11,474	$10,635	- 7.3 %
NJ	$106,737	$114,197	$81,239	- 28.9 %
NM	$20,305	$17,373	$16,999	- 2.2 %
NY	$327,699	$312,272	$278,118	- 10.9 %
NC	$71,378	$59,239	$57,964	- 2.2 %
ND	$5,942	$5,207	$5,095	- 2.1 %
OH	$127,035	$159,256	$129,430	- 18.7 %
OK	$31,210	$30,028	$24,285	- 19.1 %
OR	$34,593	$29,889	$29,246	- 2.2 %
PA	$166,516	$232,762	$175,822	- 24.5 %
RI	$28,381	$15,427	$13,882	- 10.0 %
SC	$37,145	$32,391	$31,271	- 3.5 %
SD	$7,526	$6,595	$6,453	- 2.1 %
TN	$123,571	$41,157	$40,271	- 2.2 %
TX	$293,054	$333,737	$205,425	- 38.4 %
UT	$21,219	$17,621	$16,573	- 5.9 %
VT	$7,822	$6,854	$6,706	- 2.2 %
VA	$48,665	$63,226	$48,800	- 22.8 %
WA	$55,952	$51,209	$48,936	- 4.4 %
WV	$23,446	$20,638	$20,088	- 2.7 %
WI	$57,218	$82,727	$53,069	- 35.9 %
WY	$3,962	$3,472	$3,397	- 2.1 %

HEAD START (IN THOUSANDS OF 2013 DOLLARS)

STATE	FY2011	FY2012	FY2013	CHANGE FROM '12 TO '13
AL	$122,729	$128,207	$126,860	- 1.1 %
AK	$14,184	$14,658	$14,504	- 1.1 %
AZ	$118,982	$124,158	$122,853	- 1.1 %
AR	$73,805	$76,665	$75,859	- 1.1 %
CA	$945,600	$976,936	$966,675	- 1.1 %
CO	$78,774	$82,399	$81,533	- 1.1 %
CT	$58,480	$59,919	$59,290	- 1.0 %

DE	$15,099	$15,645	$15,481	- 1.0 %
DC	$28,004	$28,418	$28,120	- 1.1 %
FL	$304,446	$319,514	$316,157	- 1.1 %
GA	$193,910	$202,529	$200,401	- 1.1 %
HI	$25,626	$26,101	$25,827	- 1.0 %
ID	$26,441	$27,792	$27,500	- 1.1 %
IL	$309,113	$320,549	$317,181	- 1.1 %
IN	$111,653	$117,504	$116,270	- 1.1 %
IA	$58,554	$60,442	$59,806	- 1.1 %
KS	$58,491	$60,984	$60,344	- 1.1 %
KY	$123,280	$127,991	$126,646	- 1.1 %
LA	$165,849	$171,307	$169,507	- 1.1 %
ME	$31,254	$32,158	$31,821	- 1.0 %
MD	$88,471	$91,164	$90,206	- 1.1 %
MA	$122,121	$125,155	$123,840	- 1.1 %
MI	$265,391	$272,968	$270,101	- 1.1 %
MN	$82,304	$85,446	$84,549	- 1.1 %
MS	$180,782	$183,886	$181,954	- 1.1 %
MO	$136,273	$141,717	$140,228	- 1.1 %
MT	$23,744	$24,461	$24,203	- 1.1 %
NE	$41,335	$43,024	$42,571	- 1.1 %
NV	$28,634	$30,553	$30,232	- 1.1 %
NH	$15,283	$15,848	$15,682	- 1.1 %
NJ	$147,188	$152,542	$150,939	- 1.1 %
NM	$60,654	$63,789	$63,119	- 1.1 %
NY	$489,959	$503,765	$498,472	- 1.1 %
NC	$165,271	$175,136	$173,297	- 1.1 %
ND	$19,671	$20,457	$20,242	- 1.0 %
OH	$281,892	$292,344	$289,273	- 1.1 %
OK	$94,373	$99,600	$98,554	- 1.1 %
OR	$68,545	$71,697	$70,943	- 1.1 %
PA	$258,902	$266,986	$264,181	- 1.1 %
RI	$24,869	$25,539	$25,271	- 1.1 %
SC	$95,957	$101,173	$100,110	- 1.1 %
SD	$21,363	$22,033	$21,802	- 1.0 %
TN	$135,513	$139,838	$138,369	- 1.1 %
TX	$548,520	$570,701	$564,706	- 1.1 %
UT	$43,769	$46,006	$45,523	- 1.1 %
VT	$15,172	$15,443	$15,281	- 1.0 %
VA	$113,260	$117,569	$116,334	- 1.1 %
WA	$115,067	$119,784	$118,526	- 1.1 %
WV	$57,512	$59,353	$58,730	- 1.0 %
WI	$103,588	$107,267	$106,140	- 1.1 %
WY	$13,648	$13,704	$13,560	- 1.1 %

Low Income Home Energy Assistance Program
(in thousands of 2013 dollars)

STATE	FY2011	FY2012	FY2013	CHANGE FROM '12 TO '13
AL	$61,096	$47,861	$39,474	- 17.5 %
AK	$14,833	$10,817	$8,549	- 21.0 %
AZ	$31,282	$22,267	$17,653	- 20.7 %
AR	$36,222	$29,011	$24,039	- 17.1 %
CA	$208,226	$155,800	$123,636	- 20.6 %
CO	$64,336	$48,093	$38,348	- 20.3 %
CT	$101,727	$80,851	$65,592	- 18.9 %
DE	$15,708	$12,155	$10,053	- 17.3 %
DC	$14,548	$10,864	$8,586	- 21.0 %
FL	$111,493	$79,313	$62,877	- 20.7 %
GA	$88,175	$62,726	$49,726	- 20.7 %
HI	$6,240	$6,208	$5,008	- 19.3 %
ID	$26,646	$19,903	$15,728	- 21.0 %
IL	$247,150	$188,764	$148,409	- 21.4 %
IN	$106,375	$81,326	$63,277	- 22.2 %
IA	$70,546	$55,722	$44,431	- 20.3 %
KS	$43,823	$32,651	$26,443	- 19.0 %
KY	$60,397	$47,194	$37,539	- 20.5 %
LA	$55,043	$44,142	$37,197	- 15.7 %
ME	$53,283	$39,160	$31,225	- 20.3 %
MD	$88,546	$70,948	$58,778	- 17.2 %
MA	$181,294	$134,879	$105,806	- 21.6 %
MI	$235,136	$175,289	$137,254	- 21.7 %
MN	$150,375	$118,777	$94,710	- 20.3 %
MS	$40,126	$32,054	$26,504	- 17.3 %
MO	$98,975	$69,363	$55,308	- 20.3 %
MT	$26,828	$20,246	$16,000	- 21.0 %
NE	$41,143	$30,709	$24,282	- 20.9 %
NV	$16,009	$11,389	$9,028	- 20.7 %
NH	$35,466	$26,487	$20,932	- 21.0 %
NJ	$187,389	$139,014	$111,275	- 20.0 %
NM	$21,300	$15,976	$12,625	- 21.0 %
NY	$513,049	$381,739	$303,168	- 20.6 %
NC	$113,147	$82,887	$68,746	- 17.1 %
ND	$27,513	$20,896	$16,513	- 21.0 %
OH	$233,366	$168,208	$132,443	- 21.3 %
OK	$44,871	$33,332	$27,776	- 16.7 %
OR	$46,432	$36,610	$29,116	- 20.5 %
PA	$290,393	$213,025	$166,027	- 22.1 %
RI	$30,751	$23,560	$18,710	- 20.6 %
SC	$48,567	$36,871	$31,338	- 15.0 %

SD	$23,687	$17,798	$14,065	- 21.0 %
TN	$74,126	$56,324	$46,087	- 18.2 %
TX	$185,535	$131,985	$104,633	- 20.7 %
UT	$32,829	$24,501	$19,350	- 21.0 %
VT	$26,583	$19,853	$15,689	- 21.0 %
VA	$106,474	$81,770	$67,196	- 17.8 %
WA	$74,311	$58,929	$46,987	- 20.3 %
WV	$40,427	$30,192	$23,860	- 21.0 %
WI	$135,360	$106,916	$85,252	- 20.3 %
WY	$12,921	$9,660	$7,631	- 21.0 %

GRANTS TO STATES FOR MEDICAID (IN THOUSANDS OF 2013 DOLLARS)

STATE	FY2011	FY2012	FY2013	CHANGE FROM '12 TO '13
AL	$3,801,769	$3,995,465	$3,925,353	- 1.8 %
AK	$928,055	$901,455	$945,031	+ 4.8 %
AZ	$6,865,928	$5,982,251	$5,883,565	- 1.6 %
AR	$3,265,650	$3,189,301	$3,314,329	+ 3.9 %
CA	$35,134,551	$27,874,293	$27,339,410	- 1.9 %
CO	$2,646,949	$2,496,594	$2,457,346	- 1.6 %
CT	$3,472,439	$3,073,121	$3,130,456	+ 1.9 %
DE	$910,633	$834,568	$856,521	+ 2.6 %
DC	$1,694,653	$1,515,011	$1,497,898	- 1.1 %
FL	$12,115,407	$11,164,975	$12,070,614	+ 8.1 %
GA	$6,118,082	$5,766,287	$5,737,216	- 0.5 %
HI	$1,017,153	$857,849	$904,755	+ 5.5 %
ID	$1,221,573	$1,268,512	$1,346,363	+ 6.1 %
IL	$8,024,831	$7,505,927	$7,380,699	- 1.7 %
IN	$5,086,275	$5,201,148	$5,198,839	- 0.0 %
IA	$2,425,528	$2,274,410	$2,336,633	+ 2.7 %
KS	$1,882,051	$1,686,241	$1,674,268	- 0.7 %
KY	$4,621,665	$4,390,099	$4,266,825	- 2.8 %
LA	$5,089,728	$5,041,920	$4,835,716	- 4.1 %
ME	$1,778,833	$1,435,515	$1,461,383	+ 1.8 %
MD	$4,446,087	$3,709,495	$3,880,423	+ 4.6 %
MA	$7,993,806	$6,935,117	$6,721,584	- 3.1 %
MI	$9,215,949	$8,672,063	$8,933,215	+ 3.0 %
MN	$5,013,460	$5,146,499	$4,985,748	- 3.1 %
MS	$3,758,313	$4,063,096	$4,284,295	+ 5.4 %
MO	$5,908,843	$6,051,756	$5,939,561	- 1.9 %
MT	$765,959	$816,063	$735,972	- 9.8 %
NE	$1,150,923	$1,091,126	$1,101,109	+ 0.9 %
NV	$1,012,210	$1,023,962	$1,062,970	+ 3.8 %
NH	$831,493	$700,521	$711,272	+ 1.5 %
NJ	$6,395,695	$5,955,090	$6,047,156	+ 1.5 %

NM	$2,708,779	$2,839,808	$3,290,363	+ 15.9 %
NY	$31,224,304	$32,083,350	$33,560,898	+ 4.6 %
NC	$7,903,429	$7,882,468	$7,778,960	- 1.3 %
ND	$507,406	$481,605	$453,344	- 5.9 %
OH	$11,449,409	$11,784,934	$11,675,254	- 0.9 %
OK	$3,204,394	$3,148,525	$3,210,651	+ 2.0 %
OR	$3,287,600	$3,179,221	$3,233,606	+ 1.7 %
PA	$13,695,289	$12,366,480	$12,469,159	+ 0.8 %
RI	$1,339,061	$1,162,527	$1,168,701	+ 0.5 %
SC	$3,923,242	$3,704,516	$3,580,296	- 3.4 %
SD	$560,705	$542,846	$536,813	- 1.1 %
TN	$6,133,038	$6,373,258	$6,861,115	+ 7.7 %
TX	$19,945,248	$18,391,382	$19,068,176	+ 3.7 %
UT	$1,444,131	$1,437,708	$1,461,234	+ 1.6 %
VT	$874,414	$871,798	$847,755	- 2.8 %
VA	$4,195,801	$3,787,219	$4,079,758	+ 7.7 %
WA	$3,807,198	$4,798,160	$5,639,378	+ 17.5 %
WV	$2,310,622	$2,268,020	$2,289,905	+ 1.0 %
WI	$4,903,615	$4,322,086	$4,441,083	+ 2.8 %
WY	$337,066	$310,131	$305,185	- 1.6 %

NATIONAL SCHOOL LUNCH (IN THOUSANDS OF 2013 DOLLARS)

STATE	FY2011	FY2012	FY2013	CHANGE FROM '12 TO '13
AL	$186,295	$194,814	$203,938	+ 4.7 %
AK	$29,960	$31,330	$32,797	+ 4.7 %
AZ	$238,242	$249,137	$260,806	+ 4.7 %
AR	$123,236	$128,872	$134,907	+ 4.7 %
CA	$1,389,099	$1,452,623	$1,520,659	+ 4.7 %
CO	$119,946	$125,431	$131,306	+ 4.7 %
CT	$81,779	$85,519	$89,524	+ 4.7 %
DE	$26,874	$28,102	$29,419	+ 4.7 %
DC	$19,406	$20,293	$21,243	+ 4.7 %
FL	$624,268	$652,817	$683,392	+ 4.7 %
GA	$433,431	$453,251	$474,480	+ 4.7 %
HI	$40,359	$42,204	$44,181	+ 4.7 %
ID	$49,828	$52,107	$54,547	+ 4.7 %
IL	$389,801	$407,626	$426,718	+ 4.7 %
IN	$225,164	$235,461	$246,489	+ 4.7 %
IA	$90,199	$94,323	$98,741	+ 4.7 %
KS	$91,352	$95,530	$100,004	+ 4.7 %
KY	$165,752	$173,333	$181,450	+ 4.7 %
LA	$196,137	$205,106	$214,713	+ 4.7 %
ME	$31,878	$33,337	$34,898	+ 4.7 %
MD	$135,051	$141,227	$147,842	+ 4.7 %

MA	$145,145	$151,782	$158,891	+ 4.7 %
MI	$274,119	$286,655	$300,081	+ 4.7 %
MN	$135,146	$141,327	$147,946	+ 4.7 %
MS	$155,512	$162,623	$170,240	+ 4.7 %
MO	$184,537	$192,976	$202,014	+ 4.7 %
MT	$24,719	$25,850	$27,060	+ 4.7 %
NE	$59,552	$62,276	$65,192	+ 4.7 %
NV	$79,834	$83,484	$87,395	+ 4.7 %
NH	$22,850	$23,895	$25,014	+ 4.7 %
NJ	$213,104	$222,849	$233,287	+ 4.7 %
NM	$84,790	$88,668	$92,820	+ 4.7 %
NY	$603,570	$631,172	$660,733	+ 4.7 %
NC	$331,458	$346,615	$362,850	+ 4.7 %
ND	$16,456	$17,209	$18,014	+ 4.7 %
OH	$322,058	$336,786	$352,560	+ 4.7 %
OK	$146,053	$152,732	$159,885	+ 4.7 %
OR	$100,747	$105,354	$110,288	+ 4.7 %
PA	$302,855	$316,706	$331,538	+ 4.7 %
RI	$26,583	$27,798	$29,100	+ 4.7 %
SC	$177,258	$185,364	$194,046	+ 4.7 %
SD	$25,878	$27,061	$28,328	+ 4.7 %
TN	$214,823	$224,646	$235,168	+ 4.7 %
TX	$1,234,964	$1,291,440	$1,351,926	+ 4.7 %
UT	$90,135	$94,257	$98,672	+ 4.7 %
VT	$13,606	$14,228	$14,894	+ 4.7 %
VA	$200,379	$209,542	$219,356	+ 4.7 %
WA	$175,098	$183,106	$191,682	+ 4.7 %
WV	$58,020	$60,673	$63,515	+ 4.7 %
WI	$154,523	$161,589	$169,158	+ 4.7 %
WY	$13,622	$14,245	$14,912	+ 4.7 %

SECTION 8 HOUSING CHOICE VOUCHERS
(IN THOUSANDS OF 2013 DOLLARS)

STATE	FY2011	FY2012	FY2013	CHANGE FROM '12 TO '13
AL	$188,866	$182,667	$186,255	+ 2.0 %
AK	$36,513	$35,314	$36,008	+ 2.0 %
AZ	$169,939	$164,362	$167,590	+ 2.0 %
AR	$102,384	$99,024	$100,968	+ 2.0 %
CA	$3,480,349	$3,366,113	$3,432,218	+ 2.0 %
CO	$242,686	$234,721	$239,330	+ 2.0 %
CT	$386,577	$373,889	$381,231	+ 2.0 %
DE	$41,155	$39,805	$40,586	+ 2.0 %
DC	$190,246	$184,002	$187,615	+ 2.0 %
FL	$885,488	$856,424	$873,243	+ 2.0 %

GA	$500,127	$483,712	$493,211	+ 2.0 %
HI	$115,306	$111,522	$113,712	+ 2.0 %
ID	$40,709	$39,373	$40,146	+ 2.0 %
IL	$913,376	$883,397	$900,745	+ 2.0 %
IN	$226,029	$218,611	$222,904	+ 2.0 %
IA	$103,015	$99,634	$101,590	+ 2.0 %
KS	$65,781	$63,621	$64,871	+ 2.0 %
KY	$197,521	$191,038	$194,790	+ 2.0 %
LA	$358,048	$346,296	$353,096	+ 2.0 %
ME	$89,003	$86,082	$87,772	+ 2.0 %
MD	$497,275	$480,954	$490,399	+ 2.0 %
MA	$887,030	$857,915	$874,763	+ 2.0 %
MI	$372,099	$359,886	$366,953	+ 2.0 %
MN	$231,791	$224,183	$228,586	+ 2.0 %
MS	$144,112	$139,383	$142,120	+ 2.0 %
MO	$252,507	$244,220	$249,015	+ 2.0 %
MT	$32,340	$31,279	$31,893	+ 2.0 %
NE	$67,664	$65,443	$66,728	+ 2.0 %
NV	$133,713	$129,324	$131,864	+ 2.0 %
NH	$87,737	$84,857	$86,523	+ 2.0 %
NJ	$699,214	$676,264	$689,544	+ 2.0 %
NM	$76,778	$74,259	$75,717	+ 2.0 %
NY	$2,402,549	$2,323,691	$2,369,324	+ 2.0 %
NC	$361,866	$349,988	$356,862	+ 2.0 %
ND	$34,323	$33,196	$33,848	+ 2.0 %
OH	$598,109	$578,477	$589,838	+ 2.0 %
OK	$135,981	$131,518	$134,100	+ 2.0 %
OR	$223,292	$215,963	$220,204	+ 2.0 %
PA	$605,085	$585,225	$596,718	+ 2.0 %
RI	$85,907	$83,087	$84,719	+ 2.0 %
SC	$149,531	$144,623	$147,463	+ 2.0 %
SD	$32,116	$31,061	$31,671	+ 2.0 %
TN	$218,461	$211,291	$215,440	+ 2.0 %
TX	$1,059,921	$1,025,131	$1,045,263	+ 2.0 %
UT	$74,832	$72,375	$73,797	+ 2.0 %
VT	$49,481	$47,856	$48,797	+ 2.0 %
VA	$396,131	$383,130	$390,653	+ 2.0 %
WA	$431,762	$417,590	$425,791	+ 2.0 %
WV	$69,028	$66,763	$68,073	+ 2.0 %
WI	$165,854	$160,411	$163,561	+ 2.0 %
WY	$13,436	$12,994	$13,250	+ 2.0 %

TEMPORARY ASSISTANCE FOR NEEDY FAMILIES -
FAMILY ASSISTANCE GRANTS (IN THOUSANDS OF 2013 DOLLARS)

STATE	FY2011	FY2012	FY2013	CHANGE FROM '12 TO '13
AL	$96,614	$91,120	$89,634	- 1.6 %
AK	$46,860	$44,196	$43,475	- 1.6 %
AZ	$207,216	$195,433	$192,246	- 1.6 %
AR	$58,739	$55,398	$54,495	- 1.6 %
CA	$3,788,749	$3,573,297	$3,515,027	- 1.6 %
CO	$140,867	$132,855	$130,689	- 1.6 %
CT	$276,219	$260,511	$256,263	- 1.6 %
DE	$33,432	$31,531	$31,017	- 1.6 %
DC	$95,884	$90,431	$88,956	- 1.6 %
FL	$582,219	$549,110	$540,156	- 1.6 %
GA	$342,434	$322,961	$317,694	- 1.6 %
HI	$102,401	$96,578	$95,003	- 1.6 %
ID	$31,488	$29,697	$29,213	- 1.6 %
IL	$605,739	$571,292	$561,976	- 1.6 %
IN	$214,109	$201,934	$198,641	- 1.6 %
IA	$135,662	$127,947	$125,861	- 1.6 %
KS	$105,534	$99,533	$97,910	- 1.6 %
KY	$187,697	$177,023	$174,136	- 1.6 %
LA	$169,768	$160,114	$157,503	- 1.6 %
ME	$80,883	$76,283	$75,039	- 1.6 %
MD	$237,197	$223,708	$220,060	- 1.6 %
MA	$475,610	$448,564	$441,249	- 1.6 %
MI	$802,762	$757,111	$744,765	- 1.6 %
MN	$272,746	$257,237	$253,042	- 1.6 %
MS	$89,835	$84,727	$83,345	- 1.6 %
MO	$224,725	$211,945	$208,489	- 1.6 %
MT	$39,384	$37,144	$36,538	- 1.6 %
NE	$59,547	$56,161	$55,245	- 1.6 %
NV	$45,460	$42,874	$42,175	- 1.6 %
NH	$39,883	$37,615	$37,002	- 1.6 %
NJ	$418,318	$394,530	$388,096	- 1.6 %
NM	$114,487	$107,977	$106,216	- 1.6 %
NY	$2,529,289	$2,385,457	$2,346,557	- 1.6 %
NC	$312,924	$295,129	$290,316	- 1.6 %
ND	$27,333	$25,778	$25,358	- 1.6 %
OH	$753,702	$710,842	$699,250	- 1.6 %
OK	$150,417	$141,863	$139,550	- 1.6 %
OR	$172,695	$162,874	$160,218	- 1.6 %
PA	$744,933	$702,572	$691,115	- 1.6 %
RI	$98,381	$92,786	$91,273	- 1.6 %

SC	$103,502	$97,616	$96,024	- 1.6 %
SD	$22,032	$20,779	$20,440	- 1.6 %
TN	$198,294	$187,018	$183,968	- 1.6 %
TX	$503,446	$474,817	$467,074	- 1.6 %
UT	$78,282	$73,831	$72,627	- 1.6 %
VT	$49,027	$46,239	$45,485	- 1.6 %
VA	$163,880	$154,561	$152,041	- 1.6 %
WA	$393,997	$371,592	$365,532	- 1.6 %
WV	$114,071	$107,584	$105,830	- 1.6 %
WI	$325,617	$307,100	$302,092	- 1.6 %
WY	$19,155	$18,066	$17,771	- 1.6 %

SPECIAL SUPPLEMENTAL NUTRITION PROGRAM FOR WOMEN, INFANTS, AND CHILDREN (WIC) (IN THOUSANDS OF 2013 DOLLARS)

STATE	FY2011	FY2012	FY2013	CHANGE FROM '12 TO '13
AL	$125,068	$122,290	$121,200	- 0.9 %
AK	$27,360	$26,752	$26,514	- 0.9 %
AZ	$156,435	$152,960	$151,597	- 0.9 %
AR	$77,375	$75,657	$74,982	- 0.9 %
CA	$1,295,652	$1,266,872	$1,255,587	- 0.9 %
CO	$78,552	$76,808	$76,123	- 0.9 %
CT	$53,103	$51,924	$51,461	- 0.9 %
DE	$18,340	$17,932	$17,773	- 0.9 %
DC	$15,553	$15,208	$15,072	- 0.9 %
FL	$381,755	$373,275	$369,950	- 0.9 %
GA	$303,590	$296,847	$294,203	- 0.9 %
HI	$35,953	$35,153	$34,841	- 0.9 %
ID	$32,310	$31,592	$31,311	- 0.9 %
IL	$251,087	$245,509	$243,322	- 0.9 %
IN	$126,261	$123,456	$122,357	- 0.9 %
IA	$52,108	$50,951	$50,497	- 0.9 %
KS	$55,273	$54,045	$53,564	- 0.9 %
KY	$121,047	$118,358	$117,304	- 0.9 %
LA	$130,695	$127,792	$126,654	- 0.9 %
ME	$20,317	$19,866	$19,689	- 0.9 %
MD	$116,662	$114,070	$113,054	- 0.9 %
MA	$94,656	$92,553	$91,729	- 0.9 %
MI	$201,148	$196,679	$194,927	- 0.9 %
MN	$108,275	$105,869	$104,927	- 0.9 %
MS	$95,570	$93,447	$92,614	- 0.9 %
MO	$103,742	$101,437	$100,534	- 0.9 %
MT	$16,559	$16,192	$16,047	- 0.9 %
NE	$36,160	$35,357	$35,042	- 0.9 %
NV	$54,102	$52,901	$52,429	- 0.9 %

NH	$12,874	$12,587	$12,475	- 0.9 %
NJ	$148,852	$145,545	$144,249	- 0.9 %
NM	$51,134	$49,998	$49,553	- 0.9 %
NY	$481,088	$470,401	$466,211	- 0.9 %
NC	$212,857	$208,128	$206,274	- 0.9 %
ND	$13,955	$13,646	$13,524	- 0.9 %
OH	$195,337	$190,999	$189,297	- 0.9 %
OK	$100,439	$98,208	$97,334	- 0.9 %
OR	$81,786	$79,970	$79,257	- 0.9 %
PA	$225,111	$220,110	$218,150	- 0.9 %
RI	$21,684	$21,203	$21,014	- 0.9 %
SC	$104,774	$102,447	$101,534	- 0.9 %
SD	$19,673	$19,236	$19,064	- 0.9 %
TN	$130,609	$127,709	$126,571	- 0.9 %
TX	$610,194	$596,639	$591,325	- 0.9 %
UT	$53,166	$51,985	$51,522	- 0.9 %
VT	$14,254	$13,937	$13,813	- 0.9 %
VA	$108,245	$105,840	$104,897	- 0.9 %
WA	$160,524	$156,959	$155,560	- 0.9 %
WV	$41,116	$40,203	$39,845	- 0.9 %
WI	$99,614	$97,401	$96,533	- 0.9 %
WY	$10,070	$9,846	$9,758	- 0.9 %

Appendix
Dashboard for the
Proposed 2013 Budget

The figures on the following six pages provide a quick reference guide for how President Obama proposes spending $3.67 trillion in fiscal year 2013, and where $2.9 trillion in projected tax revenues will come from.

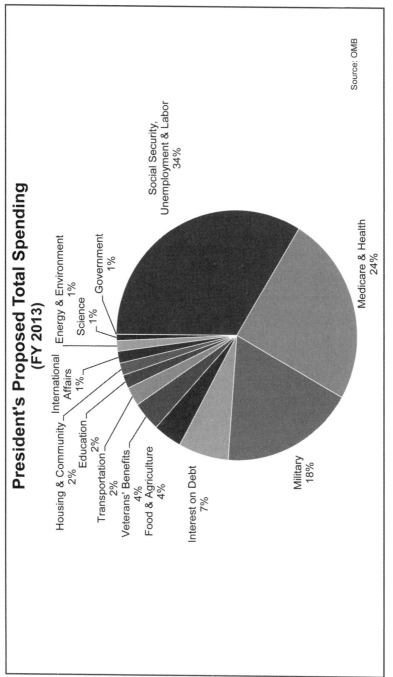

President's Proposed Total Spending (FY 2013)

Social Security, Unemployment & Labor 34%

Medicare & Health 24%

Military 18%

Interest on Debt 7%

Food & Agriculture 4%

Veterans' Benefits 4%

Transportation 2%

Education 2%

Housing & Community 2%

International Affairs 1%

Energy & Environment 1%

Science 1%

Government 1%

Source: OMB

FIGURE A.1

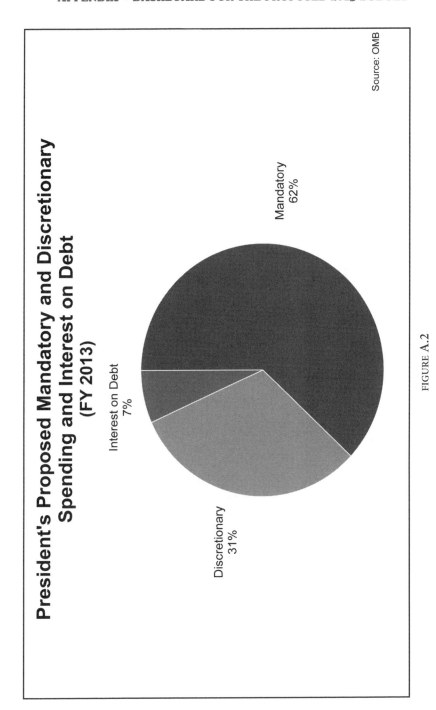

President's Proposed Mandatory and Discretionary Spending and Interest on Debt (FY 2013)

Mandatory 62%

Discretionary 31%

Interest on Debt 7%

Source: OMB

FIGURE A.2

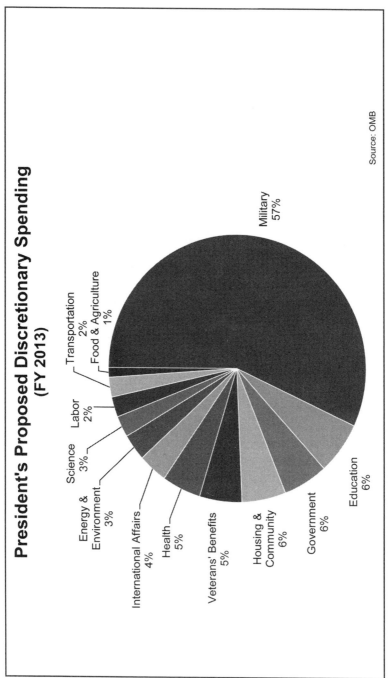

President's Proposed Discretionary Spending
(FY 2013)

Transportation
2%

Food & Agriculture
1%

Labor
2%

Science
3%

Energy &
Environment
3%

International Affairs
4%

Health
5%

Veterans' Benefits
5%

Housing &
Community
6%

Government
6%

Education
6%

Military
57%

Source: OMB

FIGURE A.3

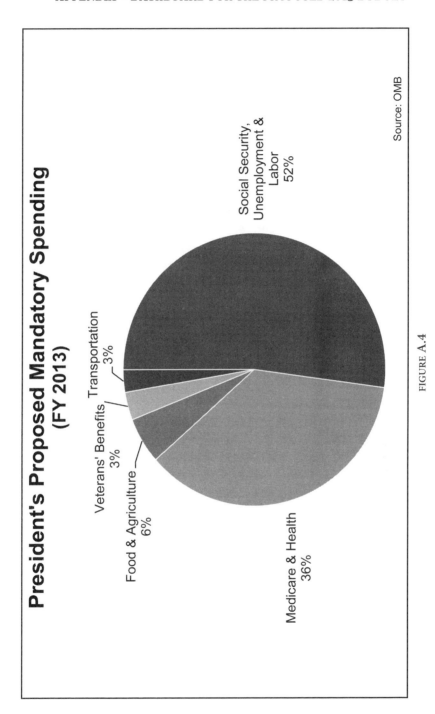

President's Proposed Mandatory Spending (FY 2013)

Source: OMB

Social Security, Unemployment & Labor 52%

Medicare & Health 36%

Food & Agriculture 6%

Veterans' Benefits 3%

Transportation 3%

FIGURE A.4

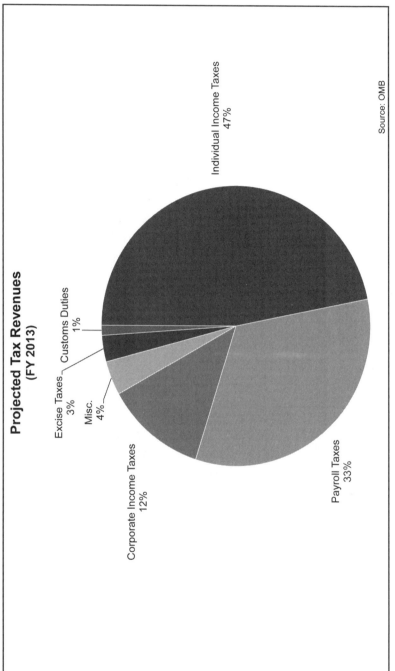

Projected Tax Revenues
(FY 2013)

Individual Income Taxes
47%

Payroll Taxes
33%

Corporate Income Taxes
12%

Misc.
4%

Excise Taxes
3%

Customs Duties
1%

Source: OMB

FIGURE A.5

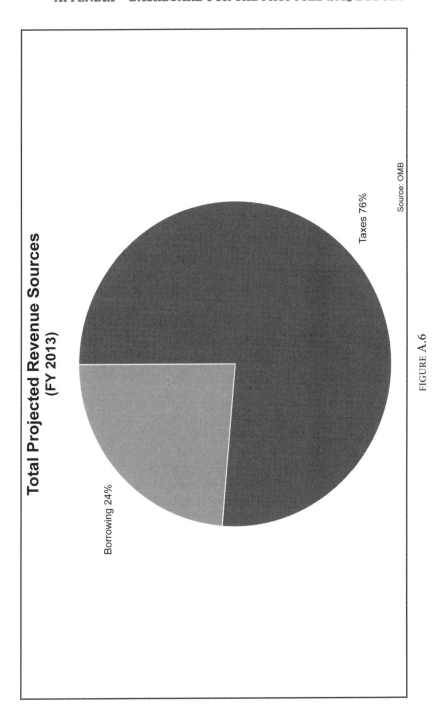

Total Projected Revenue Sources
(FY 2013)

Taxes 76%

Borrowing 24%

Source: OMB

FIGURE A.6

About National Priorities Project

National Priorities Project (NPP) is a nonprofit, nonpartisan research organization dedicated to making our complex federal budget transparent and accessible so people can exercise their right and responsibility to oversee and influence how their tax dollars are spent.

The board and staff of NPP believe that the federal budgeting process should be open and participatory, with elected officials fully accountable to their constituents. Our nation's government will only function properly if everyone participates, if all voices shape the debate. Making this a reality is crucial for a healthy and robust democracy. That's why for nearly 30 years, NPP has focused on helping people understand the impact of federal spending and revenue decision on their families and communities.

In addition to *A People's Guide to the Federal Budget*, NPP takes action in a variety of ways:

- Issuing timely and relevant reports that break down federal revenues and expenditures at the national, state, and local levels;
- Providing online seminars and participatory workshops that offer essential information about the federal budget and the budget-making process to build the capacity of our constituents;
- Maintaining a unique database which allows people to assess the personal and societal impact of federal revenue generation and spending;
- Creating highly accessible and easily sharable web-based tools that foster engagement; and
- Implementing innovative communications and networking strategies dedicated to ensuring that NPP's materials reach an increasing number and greater diversity of people and organizations.

Visit our Web site: www.nationalpriorities.org.

Like us on Facebook: http://www.facebook.com/nationalpriorities

Follow us on Twitter: https://twitter.com/natpriorities

We work for you, and people like you in local cities and towns across our nation. Our team loves to field questions or receive feedback from our constituents. Call us at 413-584-9556 or send an e-mail to info@nationalpriorities.org.

National Priorities Project Team

Staff:
Jo Comerford, Executive Director
Samantha Dana, Research Associate
Kristine Elinevsky, Director of Administration and Finance
Anders Fremstad, Research Associate
Sheila Heady, Outreach Associate
Chris Hellman, Senior Research Analyst
Osman Keshawarz, Research Associate
Mattea Kramer, Senior Research Analyst
Abby Rusk, Development Assistant
Sara Silvia, Development Officer
Brendan Smith, IT Specialist
Becky Sweger, Data Scientist and Software Developer
Ann Werboff, Research Associate

Board of Directors:
Laura Berry
Dennis Bidwell
Bill Breitbart
Savita Farooqui
Doug Hall
Jim Harper
Paul Kawika Martin
Jen Kern
Roz Lemieux
Miriam Pemberton
Lorna Peterson
Vijay Prashad
Cate Woolner

Interns:
Kyle Andrejczyk
Lauren Beatty
Nina Bellio
Lydia Bowers

Alexandra Bunnell
Molly Daniell
Isabelle D'Arcy
Noor El Edroos
Zane Farr
Rachel Jackson
Ariane Khalfa
Leila Lawrence
Mia Logg
Katrin Marquez
Jocelyn Norris
Tyler Ogden
Laras Sekarasih

National Priorities Project receives support from the following foundations:

Ben & Jerry's Foundation
Colombe Foundation
Community Foundation for the National Capital Region
Community Foundation of Western Massachusetts
Cultures of Resistance Network Foundation
DeLaCour Family Foundation
Education Foundation of America
F. Felix Foundation
Ford Foundation
Google Foundation
HKH Family Foundation
Nathan Cummings Foundation
Open Society Institute
Rockefeller Brothers Fund
Rockefeller Investment Company
Solidago Foundation
Stewart R. Mott Foundation
Sunlight Foundation
Susan A. and Donald P. Babson Charitable Foundation
Wellspring Fund of the Peace Development Fund

Glossary of Terms

Appropriation refers to a law that authorizes the expenditure of funds for a given purpose.

Appropriations Bills allocate funds to individual federal agencies. They specify how much money can be spent on a given program, and grant the government authority to enter into legal obligations that are later paid in outlays. Reviewed by the corresponding subcommittees of the Appropriations Committees in both the House and Senate, appropriations bills must also be approved by the full House and Senate before being signed by the president.

Appropriations Committees in both the House and the Senate are responsible for determining the precise levels of budget authority for all discretionary programs.

Appropriations Process is the annual process through which Congress creates the discretionary budget.

Appropriations Subcommittees in both the House and the Senate are committees made up of members of the full Appropriations Committee. Each of these subcommittees has jurisdiction over funding for a different area of the federal government. There are 12 different Appropriations subcommittees.

Authorization Bill gives a government agency the legal authority to fund and operate its programs. An authorization bill also sets maximum funding levels and includes policy guidelines. Government programs can be authorized on an annual, multi year, or permanent basis. Specific amounts authorized serve as ceilings on the amounts of money that subsequently may be appropriated, though either the House or Senate may recommend appropriating lower amounts or nothing at all.

Balanced Budget is a budget in which government revenues and government spending are equal in a given year.

Budget Authority is the federal government's legal authority to spend a given amount of money for a certain purpose, according to laws passed by Congress and the president.

Budget Resolution is a resolution passed by each house of Congress that serves as a framework for budget decisions. It sets overall spending limits but does not decide funding for specific programs.

Citizens United v. Federal Election Commission is a Supreme Court case in which the court ruled that corporations and unions have the right under the First Amendment to express political views. This decision opened the door to a vast new role for private entities to influence elections, with no limits on the amount of money they spend to do so.

Conference refers to members of the House and Senate coming together to reconcile their two different versions of a given piece of legislation.

Congressional Aides are support staff for members of Congress. They perform a variety of tasks from administrative duties to keeping track of specific policy issues.

Constituent is a person who lives in the area that an elected official represents.

Continuing Resolution extends funding for federal agencies until new appropriations bills become law.

Debt is money owed. Also see **federal debt.**

Debt Ceiling is the limit on the amount of debt the federal government allows itself to hold.

Debt Held by Federal Accounts is debt that is held by the government itself. It occurs when surpluses in federal government accounts are invested in Treasury securities.

Deficit results when government expenditures are greater than tax collections in a given year. In order to fund the deficit, the Treasury sells bonds to the public.

Direct Spending see **Mandatory Spending**

Discretionary Spending is the portion of the budget that the president requests and Congress appropriates every year. It represents roughly one-third of the total annual federal budget.

Earmarks are provisions added to legislation to designate money for a particular project, company, or organization, usually in the Congressional district of the lawmaker who sponsored it.

Effective Tax Rate is the percentage of income an individual or corporation actually pays in taxes. Effective tax rates often differ from official tax rates due to tax credits, deductions, or loopholes in the tax code.

Entitlement Programs are a type of federal program in which all people who are eligible for the program's benefits, according to eligibility rules written into law, must by law receive those benefits if they apply for them. The Supplemental Nutrition Assistance Program, commonly known as food stamps, is an example of an entitlement program; anyone who qualifies and applies for benefits receives food stamps.

Federal Debt is the sum of all past federal budget deficits, minus what that the federal government has repaid.

Federal Funds are funds collected by the federal government for general purposes, as opposed to trust funds, which are collected by the federal government for specific purposes.

Fiscal Policy refers to decisions made by the federal government regarding government spending and taxation.

Fiscal Year for the federal budget runs from October 1 through September 30. Thus, fiscal year 2013 runs from October 1, 2012, through September 30, 2013.

Gross Domestic Product (GDP) is a way of measuring the size of a nation's economy. It's the total value of all final goods and services produced in an economy in a given year. "Final" means the value of goods and services purchased by the final consumer, as opposed to the value of raw materials purchased by a factory.

House Committee on the Budget is the committee in the US House that is responsible for writing a budget resolution, among other responsibilities. It became a standing committee with the passage of the Congressional Budget and Impoundment Control Act of 1974.

Inflation is an increase in the average price level in an economy.

Interest is the fee paid by a borrower to a lender, usually expressed as a percentage of the amount borrowed.

Interest on Debt is the interest payments the federal government makes on its accumulated debt, minus interest income received by the government for assets it owns.

Lobbying is the act of trying to influence lawmakers.

Mandatory Spending is federal money that is spent based on existing laws that govern particular programs, such as entitlement programs like Social Security or food stamps. Mandatory spending is *not* part of the annual appropriations process.

Marginal Tax Rate is the rate at which your last dollar of income is taxed. So, if you make $22,000 per year, then your first $8,500 of income is taxed at a rate of 10 percent, and the rest of your income is taxed at 15 percent. In that case, 15 percent is your marginal tax rate.

Medicare is a federal program that provides health care coverage for senior citizens and the disabled. It is funded through payroll taxes.

Monetary Policy refers to actions by the Federal Reserve Bank to influence the supply of money in the economy as well as interest rates.

Multiplier Effect is an economics term for an increase in national income that is greater than the initial increase in spending that caused it.

Nominal dollar amounts are not adjusted for inflation; they are the cost or value of something expressed as its price in the year it was purchased. For example, if in 2006 you paid $9 for a movie ticket, then the ticket's nominal price is $9.

Obligations are binding financial agreements entered into by the federal government. Examples of obligations include contracts, purchase orders, and the hiring of federal workers.

Opportunity Cost is what you give up when making a decision, measured in terms of the next best alternative.

Outlays are money paid out by the US Treasury; they occur when obligations are actually paid off, primarily by issuing checks or making electronic fund transfers.

Payroll Taxes are taxes paid jointly by employers and employees. Payroll taxes fund the Social Security and Medicare programs.

Per Capita means "per person." For example, per capita GDP is GDP divided by population, which shows GDP on a per-person basis.

Poverty Line, also called poverty level or the poverty threshold, is determined by annual income. For example, the poverty line for a family of four was $22,113 in 2010; any family of four earning that amount or less was considered to be in poverty.

Progressive describes a tax system in which wealthier people pay a higher percentage of their income in taxes than lower-income people. Progressive also describes political ideology on the left side of the political spectrum.

Real numbers have been adjusted for inflation.

Regressive refers to a tax system in which people earning lower incomes pay a higher percentage of their income in taxes than their wealthier counterparts.

Senate Committee on the Budget is the committee in the US Senate that is responsible for writing a budget resolution, among other responsibilities. It became a standing committee with the passage of the Congressional Budget and Impoundment Control Act of 1974.

Sequestration is automatic cuts to spending.

Social Security, officially called the Old Age, Survivors, and Disability Insurance program, is a federal program that is meant to ensure that elderly and disabled people do not live in poverty. It is funded through payroll taxes.

Subsidy is direct assistance from the federal government to individuals or businesses, which helps defray the costs of certain activities.

Supplemental Appropriation is legislation that provides funding beyond what was appropriated in the normal appropriations process. Congress generally passes supplemental appropriations in response to emergencies like natural disasters or other kinds of urgent circumstances.

Surplus is the amount by which revenues exceed expenditures in the federal budget. The federal government has only run a surplus in four years in the last half century, from 1998 to 2001.

Trust Funds are funds collected by the federal government for specific purposes, as designated by law. For example, payroll taxes are trust funds collected by the federal government to pay for the Social Security and Medicare programs.

List of Figures

Chapter 2. The Big Picture
2.1 The Connection Between Budget Authority and Outlays
2.2 Nominal Outlays and Real Outlays
2.3 CHIP Spending Per Child and Per Participant

Chapter 3. A Brief History of the Federal Budget
3.1 The Evolving Federal Budget
3.2 The Statistical Abstract
3.3 Federal Spending as Percent of GDP
3.4 Mandatory and Discretionary Spending and Interest on Debt

Chapter 4. Who Decides the Federal Budget?
4.1 The Three Branches of Government
4.2 Annual Budget Process
4.3 Annual Budget Process Flow Chart

Chapter 5. Where Does the Money Come From?
5.1 All Revenues by Source
5.2 Marginal Tax Rates by Income Level
5.3 Individual and Corporate Income Taxes as Percent of All Federal Revenues
5.4 Corporate Taxes as Percent of GDP in OECD Countries
5.5 Tax Brackets in 1955
5.6 Federal Taxes on Your Paystub

Chapter 6. Where Does the Money Go?
6.1 All Federal Revenue and Spending in 2011
6.2 Total Federal Spending
6.3 Mandatory and Discretionary Spending and Interest on Debt
6.4 Discretionary Spending
6.5 Mandatory Spending
6.6 Where Your 2011 Income Tax Dollar Went
6.7 Federal Income Tax Receipt
6.8 Federal Spending as Percent of GDP
6.9 Military and Nonmilitary Discretionary Spending

6.10 Federal Spending by Category Over Time

Chapter 7. The Federal Debt
7.1 Revenues, Outlays, Deficits, and Surpluses
7.2 Deficits and Surpluses
7.3 Federal Debt as Percent of GDP
7.4 Federal Debt in Dollars and as Percent of GDP
7.5 The Federal Debt in Dollars
7.6 US Debt Held by the Public
7.7 Federal Debt Held in Federal Accounts
7.8 Interest on Debt as Percent of Total Federal Spending
7.9 Raising the Debt Ceiling
7.10 Deficit Control Policies

Chapter 8. The President's 2013 Budget Request
8.1 Two Decades of the Federal Budget
8.2 President's Proposed Total Spending
8.3 Discretionary Spending in the President's 2013 Budget
8.4 Mandatory Spending in the President's 2013 Budget
8.5 Projected Tax Revenues
8.6 Total Projected Revenue Sources
8.7 Medicare & Health as Percent of Total Federal Spending
8.8 Comparison of Funding Projections for the Department of Defense in the 2012 and 2013 Budgets
8.9 Education as Percent of Total Federal Spending

Chapter 9. Take Action
9.1 Opportunities to Take Action

Appendix: Dashboard for the Proposed 2013 Budget
A.1 President's Proposed Total Spending
A.2 President's Proposed Mandatory and Discretionary Spending and Interest on Debt
A.3 President's Proposed Discretionary Spending
A.4 President's Proposed Mandatory Spending
A.5 Projected Tax Revenues
A.6 Total Projected Revenue

List of Extras

Chapter 1. Why Should You Care About the Federal Budget?
Democracy

Chapter 3. A Brief History of the Federal Budget
Key Government Agencies Involved in the Federal Budget

Chapter 4. Who Decides the Federal Budget?
The Three Branches of Government
What Are Appropriations "Subcommittees"?
The "Chair's Mark" and Majority Power
All About Earmarks

Chapter 5. Where Does the Money Come From?
The Buffet Rule

Chapter 6. Where Does the Money Go?
Helping People and the Economy
Budget Trade-Offs
Major Social Programs Funded in the Federal Budget

Chapter 7. The Federal Debt
Does the Federal Debt Affect You?
Are Deficits Bad?

Chapter 9. Take Action
Timing Is Everything

List of Learn to Fish

Chapter 5. Where Does the Money Come From?
Do We Tax Corporations a Lot or a Little?
Do Some People Pay No Taxes at All?

Chapter 6. Where Does the Money Go?
The Politics of Measuring Federal Spending

Chapter 7. The Federal Debt
Why Measure the Federal Debt as a Percent of GDP?

Chapter 8. The President's 2013 Budget Request
When You Assume…

List of Did You Knows

Chapter 2. The Big Picture
The Secret Service Was Created to Prevent Inflation

Chapter 3. A Brief History of the Federal Budget
The Hamilton-Burr Duel
The Statistical Abstract of the United States
A Second Bill of Rights

Chapter 4. Who Decides the Federal Budget?
The President's Budget Assumes All Sorts of Things
How the Federal Government Funds Emergencies
There Are More Than Two Political Parties
Most Countries Have Publicly Financed Elections

Chapter 5. Where Does the Money Come From?
There's an Excise Tax for Bronzing Up at the Tanning Salon
The Earned Income Tax Credit
The Size of the Bush Tax Cuts
The Tax Code Plays Favorites

Chapter 6. Where Does the Money Go?
How Big Is One Trillion Dollars?

Chapter 7. The Federal Debt
How Big Is the Federal Debt?

Chapter 8. The President's 2013 Budget Request
How Many Miles is the Pentagon Budget?

Endnotes

1   Suzanne Mettler, "Our Hidden Government Benefits," *The New York Times*, September 19, 2011. January 2, 2012 (http://www.nytimes.com/2011/09/20/opinion/our-hidden-government-benefits.html).

2   Jeffrey M. Jones, "Americans Say Federal Gov't Wastes Over Half of Every Tax Dollar," *Gallup*, September 19, 2011. January 9, 2012 (http://www.gallup.com/poll/149543/americans-say-federal-gov-wastes-half-every-dollar.aspx).

3   Ed Goeas and Nicholas Thompson, "Key Findings from National Survey," The Terrance Group, March 1, 2011. January 9, 2012 (www.politico.com/pdf/PPM191_poll.pdf).

4   Opinion Research Corporation, "CNN Opinion Research Poll," January 25, 2011. January 9, 2012 (http://i2.cdn.turner.com/cnn/2011/images/01/25/rel2d.pdf).

5   *Merriam-Webster Dictionary*, "Democracy," January 9, 2012 (http://www.merriam-webster.com/dictionary/democracy).

6   Steven Kull et al., "How the American Public Would Deal with the Budget Deficit," Program for Public Consultation, February 3, 2012 (http://www.worldpublicopinion.org/pipa/articles/brunitedstatescanadara/677.php).

7   US Government Printing Office, "Budget of the United States Government: Citizens Guide to the Federal Budget," January 28, 2010. January 9, 2012 (http://www.gpoaccess.gov/usbudget/citizensguide.html).

8   Office of Management and Budget, "Budget of the United States Government, Fiscal Year 2013," February 13, 2012.

9   Rob Crotty, "What's In Your Wallet?" TheNationalArchives.gov, 3 November 2010. January 13, 2012 (http://blogs.archives.gov/prologue/?p=2376).

[10] Office of Management and Budget, "Analytical Perspectives, Budget of the United States Government, Fiscal Year 2012," February 14, 2011.

[11] US Department of the Treasury, "History of the Treasury," January 6, 2012 (http://www.treasury.gov/about/history/Pages/edu_history_brochure.aspx).

[12] Ibid.

[13] Ibid.

[14] Library of Congress, "Today in History: July 11." January 10, 2012 (http://memory.loc.gov/ammem/today/jul11.html).

[15] US Department of the Treasury, "History of the Treasury," January 6, 2012 (http://www.treasury.gov/about/history/Pages/edu_history_brochure.aspx).

[16] O'Neill, June E., director, Congressional Budget Office, "Congressional Budget Process," Statement before the Subcommittee on Legislative and Budget Process and the Subcommittee on Rules and Organization of the House, Committee on Rules, US House of Representatives, July 13, 1995. November 7, 2011 (http://www.cbo.gov/doc.cfm?index=5500&type=0).

[17] Statistical Abstract of the United States, "Historical Statistics of the United States, 1789–1945," Series P 99-108, Federal Government Finances: Treasury Expenditures: 1789–1945. November 18, 2011 (http://www2.census.gov/prod2/statcomp/documents/HistoricalStatisticsoftheUnitedStates1789–1945.pdf).

[18] O'Neill, "Congressional Budget Process."

[19] US Census Bureau, "What is the Statistical Abstract?" January 6, 2012 (http://www.census.gov/compendia/statab/).

[20] US Treasury Department, *Statistical Abstract of the United States*, 1878 (Government Printing Office, 1879), 153–157.

[21] US Census Bureau, "What is the Statistical Abstract?"

[22] Office of Management and Budget, Historical Table 1.2—Summary of Receipts, Outlays, and Surpluses or Deficits as Percentages of GDP: 1930–2016, February 14, 2011.

[23] Franklin D. Roosevelt American Heritage Center Museum, "The Economic Bill of Rights," 2007. January 13, 2012 (http://www.fdrheritage.org/bill_of_rights.htm).

[24] National Archives, "Teaching With Documents: FDR's First Inaugural Address, Declaring 'War' on the Great Depression," November 10, 2011 (http://www.archives.gov/education/lessons/fdr-inaugural/).

[25] Ibid.

[26] Office of Management and Budget, Historical Table 1.1—Summary of Receipts, Outlays, and Surpluses or Deficits: 1789–2016, February 14, 2011

[27] Office of Management and Budget, Historical Table 1.2—Summary of Receipts, Outlays, and Surpluses or Deficits as Percentages of GDP: 1930–2016, February 14, 2011.

[28] Lyndon B. Johnson, "Annual Message to the Congress on the State of the Union," January 8, 1964. November 10, 2011 (http://www.lbjlib.utexas.edu/johnson/archives.hom/speeches.hom/640 108.asp).

[29] O'Neill, "Congressional Budget Process."

[30] Ibid.

[31] Office of Management and Budget, Historical Table 1.2—Summary of Receipts, Outlays, and Surpluses or Deficits as Percentages of GDP: 1930–2016, February 14, 2011.

[32] Megan Suzanne Lynch, "Statutory Budget Controls in Effect Between 1985 and 2002," Congressional Research Service Report R41901, July 1, 2011. November 8, 2011 (www.fas.org/sgp/crs/misc/R41901.pdf).

33 Marc Labonte and Mindy R. Levit, "The Budget Control Act of 2011: Effects on Spending Levels and the Budget Deficit," Congressional Research Service Report R42013, November 29, 2011. January 6, 2012 (http://www.fas.org/sgp/crs/misc/R42013.pdf).

34 US Constitution, article 1, section 8, clause 1.

35 Congressional Research Service, "Introduction to the Federal Budget Process," Report 98–721, December 2, 2010.

36 Congressional Research Service, "Overview of the Authorization-Appropriations Process," Report 20–731, June 17, 2008.

37 United States Senate Committee on Appropriations, "The Budget Process." December 9, 2011 (http://appropriations.senate.gov/about-budget-process.cfm).

38 Congressional Research Service, "Mandatory Spending: Evolution and Growth Since 1962," Report 33–074, September 13, 2005.

39 Congressional Research Service, "American National Government: An Overview," Report RS20443, May 20, 2003.

40 Congressional Research Service, "Introduction to the Federal Budget Process," Report 98–721, December 2, 2010.

41 US Constitution, article 1, section 7, clause 2.

42 Congressional Research Service, "Introduction to the Federal Budget Process," Report 98–721, December 2, 2010.

43 Congressional Research Service, "The Role of the President in Budget Development," Report 20–179, August 28, 2003.

44 Congressional Research Service, "Introduction to the Federal Budget Process."

45 Ibid.

[46] Office of Management and Budget, "Analytical Perspectives, Budget of the United States Government, Fiscal Year 2012," Table 27–4, February 14, 2011.

[47] Congressional Research Service, "The Congressional Research Service and the American Legislative Process." Report 33–471, April 12, 2011.

[48] Congressional Research Service, "Introduction to the Federal Budget Process."

[49] Congressional Research Service, "The Congressional Budget Process: A Brief Overview," Report 20–095, January 28, 2004.

[50] US Constitution, article 1, section 7, clause 1.

[51] Congressional Research Service, "The Appropriations Process: An Introduction," Report 97–684, February 22, 2007.

[52] Congressional Research Service, "The Congressional Budget Process: A Brief Overview," Report 20–095, January 28, 2004.

[53] The Library of Congress, "Jurisdictional Changes in House & Senate Appropriations Subcommittees," January 9, 2012 (http://thomas.loc.gov/home/approp/jurischgs.html).

[54] Congressional Research Service, "The Appropriations Process: An Introduction."

[55] Congressional Research Service, "Introduction to the Federal Budget Process."

[56] House of Representatives Committee on Rules, "About the Committee on Rules," January 9, 2012 (http://rules.house.gov/singlepages.aspx?newsid=1&rsbd=4).

[57] Congressional Research Service, "The Congressional Budget Process: A Brief Overview."

58 *The New York Times*, "Pork? That? What do you mean?" August 1, 2011. November 17, 2011 (http://www.nytimes.com/2011/08/02/opinion/pork-earmarks-what-do-you-mean.html?_r=1&ref=earmarks).

59 Open Secrets, "111ᵗʰ Congress Earmarks." November 28, 2011 (http://www.opensecrets.org/earmarks/).

60 Congressional Research Service, "Continuing Resolutions: Latest Action and Brief Overview of Recent Practices," Report 30–343, April 26, 2011.

61 Congressional Research Service, "Disaster Relief Funding and Emergency Supplemental Appropriations," Report 40–708, May 24, 2010.

62 Congressional Research Service, "Congressional Oversight: An Overview," Report 41–079, February 22, 2010.

63 *The New York Times*, "For Republican Freshmen, the Power of Saying No," July 29, 2011. January 9, 2012 (http://www.nytimes.com/2011/07/30/us/politics/30freshmen.html).

64 Committee on House Administration, "Congressional Member and Staff Organizations," January 9, 2012 (http://cha.house.gov/member-services/congressional-memberstaff-organizations).

65 Congressional Research Service, "Structure and Functions of the Federal Reserve System," Report 20–826, November 10, 2010.

66 Joint Economic Committee Republicans, "Spend Less, Owe Less, Grow the Economy," March 15, 2011. January 14, 2012 (http://www.speaker.gov/UploadedFiles/JEC_Jobs_Study.pdf).

67 Paul Johnson, "A Glossary of Political Economy Terms: Supply Side Economics," January 10, 2012 (http://www.auburn.edu/~johnspm/gloss/supply_side).

68 The Associated Press, "GOP: Offsetting Cuts Must Cover Payroll Tax Relief," November 30, 2011. December 22, 2011 (http://www.npr.org/templates/story/story.php?storyId=142941533).

[69]   Alan Blinder, "The Concise Encyclopedia of Economics: Keynesian Economics," January 10, 2012, (http://www.econlib.org/library/Enc/KeynesianEconomics.html).

[70]   Quinnipiac University, "Campaign Finance Reform Would 'Clean Up' Government, Connecticut Voters Tell Quinnipiac College Poll; But Dems, Republicans Split on Using Tax Dollars," February 18, 2000. January 10, 2012 (http://www.quinnipiac.edu/institutes-and-centers/polling-institute/connecticut/release-detail?ReleaseID=559).

[71]   The Sunlight Foundation, "The Political One Percent of the One Percent," December 13, 2011. December 22, 2011 (http://sunlightfoundation.com/blog/2011/12/13/the-political-one-percent-of-the-one-percent/).

[72]   Ibid.

[73]   *The New York Times*, "Times Topics: Campaign Finance," June 18, 2011. December 22, 2011 (http://topics.nytimes.com/top/reference/timestopics/subjects/c/campaign_finance/index.html?scp=1&sq=citizens%20united&st=cse).

[74] International Foundation for Electoral Systems, "Global Trends in the Regulation of Political Finance," February 2011. January 9, 2012 (http://www.ifes.org/Content/Publications/White-Papers/2011/~/media/Files/Publications/White%20PaperReport/2011/IPSA_conference_paper_ohman.pdf).

[75]   Congressional Research Service, "Lobbying Congress: An Overview of Legal Provisions and Congressional Ethics Rules," Report 31–126, 24 Oct. 2007.

[76]   Center for Responsive Politics, "Lobbying Database," November 30, 2011 (http://www.opensecrets.org/lobby/index.php).

[77]   Census Bureau, "Apportionment Data," January 9, 2012 (http://2010.census.gov/2010census/data/apportionment-data-text.php).

[78]   Tip O'Neill, *All Politics is Local and Other Rules of the Game* (Holbrook: Bob Adams Press, 1994).

79 Congressional Budget Office, "The Budget and Economic Outlook: Fiscal Years 2011 to 2021," January 2011. January 9, 2012 (http://www.cbo.gov/ftpdocs/120xx/doc12039/01-26_fy2011outlook.pdf).

80 Office of Management and Budget, "Budget of the United States Government, Fiscal Year 2013," February 13, 2012.

81 Government Printing Office, "Patient Protection and Affordable Care Act," January 7, 2012 (http://www.gpo.gov/fdsys/pkg/PLAW-111publ148/pdf/PLAW-111publ148.pdf).

82 Internal Revenue Service, "Data Book 2007," November 29, 2011 (http://www.irs.gov/pub/irs-soi/07dbreturnfiled.pdf).

83 Internal Revenue Service, "2011 Tax Rate Schedules," January 7, 2012 (http://www.irs.gov/pub/irs-pdf/i1040tt.pdf?portlet=103).

84 Tax Policy Center, "Taxation and the Family: What is the Earned Income Tax Credit?" February 5, 2010. January 9, 2012 (http://www.taxpolicycenter.org/briefing-book/key-elements/family/eitc.cfm).

85 Internal Revenue Service, "Earned Income Tax Credit Questions and Answers," December 16, 2011. January 9, 2012 (http://www.irs.gov/individuals/article/0,,id=96466,00.html).

86 Tax Policy Center, "Taxation and the Family: What Is the Child Tax Credit?" February 4, 2010. January 9, 2012 (http://www.taxpolicycenter.org/briefing-book/key-elements/family/ctc.cfm).

87 National Priorities Project, "What the Tax Cuts Cost," December 22, 2011(http://www.costoftaxcuts.com/about/).

88 Office of Management and Budget, Historical Table 4.1—Outlays by Agency: 1962–2016, February 14, 2011.

89 Internal Revenue Service, "Publication 542: Corporations," November 11, 2011 (http://www.irs.gov/pub/irs-pdf/p542.pdf).

90 Congressional Research Service, "An Analysis of the 'Buffet Rule,'" Report R42043, October 7, 2011.

91 Citizens for Tax Justice, "Top Federal Income Tax Rates Since 1913," November 2011. January 9, 2012 (http://www.ctj.org/pdf/regcg.pdf).

92 Citizens for Tax Justice, "Corporate Taxpayers & Corporate Tax Dodgers," November 2011. November 29, 2011 (http://www.ctj.org/ctjreports/2011/11/corporate_taxpayers_corporate_tax_dodgers_2008-2010.php).

93 Ibid.

94 Ibid.

95 Ibid.

96 Congressional Budget Office, "Corporate Income Tax Rates: International Comparisons," November 11, 2011 (http://www.cbo.gov/ftpdocs/69xx/doc6902/11-28-CorporateTax.pdf).

97 Tax Foundation, "U.S. Federal Income Tax Rates History, 1913–2011," December 15, 2011 (http://www.taxfoundation.org/publications/show/151.html).

98 Center on Budget and Policy Priorities, "The Decline of Corporate Income Tax Revenues," December 15, 2011 (http://www.cbpp.org/files/10-16-03tax.pdf).

99 Citizens for Tax Justice, "Corporate Taxpayers & Corporate Tax Dodgers."

100 Congressional Budget Office, "Percent of Households Paying More in Payroll Taxes Than Income Taxes (2007)," November 23, 2011 (http://www.cbo.gov/publications/collections/tax/2010/paying_more_payroll.pdf).

101 Social Security Administration, "Contribution and Benefit Base," January 8, 2012 (http://www.ssa.gov/oact/COLA/cbb.html).

102 Office of Management and Budget, Historical Table 3.2—Outlays by Function and Subfunction: 1962–2016, February 14, 2011.

[103] Kenneth Hanson, "Food Stamps Provide Fiscal Stimulus," *Amber Waves* (United States Department of Agriculture Economic Research Service: April 2008), 12 January 2012 (http://www.ers.usda.gov/amberwaves/april08/findings/foodstamp.htm).

[104] US Census Bureau, *Historical Statistics of the United States 1789–1945*, Series P 99–108: Federal Government Finances—Treasury Expenditures: 1789–1945.

[105] Ibid.

[106] Office of Management and Budget, Historical Table 1.2—Summary of Receipts, Outlays, and Surpluses or Deficits as Percentages of GDP: 1930–2016, February 14, 2011.

[107] Lyndon B. Johnson, "Annual Message to the Congress on the State of the Union," January 8, 1964. November 10, 2011 (http://www.lbjlib.utexas.edu/johnson/archives.hom/speeches.hom/640108.asp).

[108] The White House, "The Clinton Presidency: Historic Economic Growth." December 22, 2011 (http://clinton5.nara.gov/WH/Accomplishments/eightyears-03.html).

[109] US Department of Health and Human Services, "2008 Indicators of Welfare Dependence." December 22, 2011 (http://aspe.hhs.gov/hsp/indicators08/apa.shtml#ttanf4).

[110] US Department of Health and Human Services, "2008 Indicators of Welfare Dependence: Table TANF 4." December 22, 2011 (http://aspe.hhs.gov/hsp/indicators08/apa.shtml#ttanf4).

[111] National Priorities Project. "Cost of War: About." January 10, 2012 (http://costofwar.com/en/about/counters/).

[112] Office of Management and Budget, Public Budget Database: Outlays, February 13, 2012.

[113] Recovery.gov: Track the Money, "The Recovery Act." November 18, 2011 (http://www.recovery.gov/About/Pages/The_Act.aspx).

[114] Congressional Budget Office, "Report on the Troubled Asset Relief Program," March 2011. January 11, 2012 (http://www.cbo.gov/ftpdocs/121xx/doc12118/03-29-TARP.pdf).

[115] Office of Management and Budget, "Historical Table 3.2: Outlays by Function and Subfunction: 1962–2016," February 14, 2011.

[116] Internal Revenue Service, "Individual Income Tax Statistics—Zip Code Data." *Note: Data and Web site are currently under internal review by the IRS.*

[117] US Census Bureau, "American Community Population Survey Supplement," March 2008.

[118] US Department of Health and Human Services, "Head Start Program Fact Sheet Fiscal Year 2009," February 2011. January 15, 2012 (http://eclkc.ohs.acf.hhs.gov/hslc/mr/factsheets/eHeadStartProgr.htm).

[119] US Census Bureau, "American Community Survey: Health Insurance Coverage Status by Age for the Civilian Noninstitutionalized Population," March 2008.

[120] US Department of Health and Human Services, "2008 Actuarial Report on the Financial Outlook for Medicaid," October 17, 2008. January 15, 2012 (https://www.cms.gov/ActuarialStudies/downloads/MedicaidReport2008.pdf).

[121] US Census Bureau, "American Community Survey: School Enrollment by Level of School for the Population 3 Years and Over," March 2008.

[122] Bureau of Labor Statistics, "Occupational Employment Statistics," May 2008.

[123] US Department of Health and Human Services, "Head Start Program Fact Sheet," January 6, 2012 (http://www.acf.hhs.gov/programs/ohs/about/fy2010.html).

[124] Ibid.

[125] US Department of Health and Human Services, "About the Office of Head Start," January 6, 2012 (http://www.acf.hhs.gov/programs/ohs/about/index.html#mission).

[126] US Department of Health and Human Services, "ACF Questions and Answers Support: Eligibility," August 16, 2007. January 14, 2012 (http://faq.acf.hhs.gov/).

[127] Congressional Research Service, "The Low Income Home Energy Assistance Program (LIHEAP): Program and Funding," Report RL31865, January 13, 2011.

[128] US Department of Health and Human Services, "Fact Sheet," January 6, 2012 (http://www.acf.hhs.gov/programs/ocs/liheap/about/factsheet.html).

[129] US Department of Health and Human Services, "Instructions for Completing the *LIHEAP Household Report for FFY2011*," July 25, 2011. January 6, 2012 (http://www.acf.hhs.gov/programs/ocs/liheap/forms/hhrptins.doc).

[130] US Department of Health and Human Services, "Eligibility Criteria," January 6, 2012 (http://www.acf.hhs.gov/programs/ocs/liheap/guidance/eligibility.html).

[131] Centers for Medicare and Medicaid Services, "Overview," January 6, 2012 (https://www.cms.gov/history/).

[132] Centers for Medicare and Medicaid Services, "MSIS State Summary FY 2009," October 10, 2011.

[133] US Social Security Administration, "Medicaid Information," January 6, 2012 (http://www.ssa.gov/disabilityresearch/wi/medicaid.htm).

[134] Centers for Medicare and Medicaid Services, "Medicaid and CHIP Program Information by Population," January 6, 2012 (http://www.medicaid.gov/Medicaid-CHIP-Program-Information/By-Population/By-Population.html).

[135] Centers for Medicare and Medicaid Services, "Mandatory Eligibility Groups," January 6, 2012

(https://www.cms.gov/MedicaidEligibility/03_MandatoryEligibilityGroups.asp#TopOfPage).

[136] Centers for Medicare and Medicaid Services, "Overview," January 6, 2012.

[137] *Medicare and Medicaid Research Review*, "The Medicare and Medicaid Statistical Supplement: Table 2.8," July 1, 2010.

[138] Centers for Medicare and Medicaid Services, "Medicare Eligibility Tool," January 6, 2012 (http://www.medicare.gov/MedicareEligibility/home.asp?dest=NAV%7CHome%7CGeneralEnrollment&version=default&browser=Chrome%7C15%7CWinXP&language=English).

[139] US Department of Agriculture, "National School Lunch Program," January 6, 2012 (http://www.fns.usda.gov/cnd/lunch/).

[140] Ibid.

[141] Food Research and Action Center, "National School Lunch Program," January 6, 2012 (http://frac.org/federal-foodnutrition-programs/school-breakfast-and-lunch/national-school-lunch-program/).

[142] US Department of Agriculture, "National School Lunch Program," January 6, 2012 (http://www.fns.usda.gov/cnd/lunch/).

[143] Food Research and Action Center, "National School Lunch Program," January 6, 2012 (http://frac.org/wp-content/uploads/2010/08/fedrates.pdf).

[144] American Association of Community Colleges, "Fall 2011: Estimated Headcount Enrollment and Pell Grant Trends," January 6, 2012 (http://aacc.nche.edu/Publications/Reports/Documents/Headcount_Enrollment.pdf).

[145] US Department of Education, "Federal Pell Grant Program," January 6, 2012 (http://www2.ed.gov/programs/fpg/index.html).

[146] Ibid.

[147] US Department of Housing and Urban Development, "Section 8 Program Background Information," January 6, 2012 (http://portal.hud.gov/hudportal/HUD?src=/program_offices/housing/mfh/rfp/s8bkinfo).

[148] Center on Budget and Policy Priorities, "Rental Assistance is Effective But Serves Only a Fraction of Eligible Household," January 6, 2012 (http://www.cbpp.org/files/2-24-09hous-sec2.pdf).

[149] US Department of Housing and Urban Development, "Housing Choice Vouchers Fact Sheet," January 6, 2012 (http://portal.hud.gov/hudportal/HUD?src=/topics/housing_choice_voucher_program_section_8).

[150] US Department of Housing and Urban Development, "Project Based Vouchers," January 6, 2012 (http://portal.hud.gov/hudportal/HUD?src=/program_offices/public_indian_housing/programs/hcv/project).

[151] US Department of Housing and Urban Development, "Housing Choice Vouchers Fact Sheet," January 6, 2012.

[152] Social Security Administration, "Historical Background and Development of Social Security," January 6, 2012 (http://www.ssa.gov/history/briefhistory3.html).

[153] Social Security Online, "Beneficiary Data: Number of Social Security Beneficiaries," January 19, 2011. January 12, 2012 (http://www.ssa.gov/oact/ProgData/icpGraph.html).

[154] Social Security Administration, "Understanding the Benefits," January 6, 2012 (http://www.socialsecurity.gov/pubs/10024.html).

[155] Ibid.

[156] US Department of Agriculture, "History of the WIC Program," January 6, 2012 (http://www.ers.usda.gov/publications/fanrr27/fanrr27c.pdf).

[157] US Department of Agriculture, "WIC Program Participation and Costs," January 5, 2012. January 6, 2012 (http://www.fns.usda.gov/pd/wisummary.htm).

[158] US Department of Agriculture, "WIC At A Glance," January 6, 2012 (http://www.fns.usda.gov/wic/aboutwic/wicataglance.htm).

[159] US Department of Agriculture, "WIC Prescreening Tool," January 6, 2012 (https://stars.fns.usda.gov/wps/pages/start.jsf).

[160] US Department of Agriculture, "WIC Eligibility Requirements," January 6, 2012 (http://www.fns.usda.gov/wic/howtoapply/eligibilityrequirements.htm).

[161] US Department of Agriculture, "WIC Income Eligibility Guidelines 2011–2012," January 6, 2012 (http://www.fns.usda.gov/wic/howtoapply/incomeguidelines.htm).

[162] US Department of Agriculture, "The State Children's Health Insurance Program (SCHIP)," January 6, 2012 (http://www.fns.usda.gov/cnd/SCHIP/factsheet.htm).

[163] Insure Kids Now, "Number of Children Ever Enrolled in Medicaid and Chip," January 6, 2012 (http://www.insurekidsnow.gov/professionals/reports/chipra/2010_enrollment_data.pdf).

[164] US Department of Agriculture, "The State Children's Health Insurance Program (SCHIP)," January 6, 2012 (http://www.fns.usda.gov/cnd/SCHIP/factsheet.htm).

[165] Ibid.

[166] US Department of Agriculture, "A Short History of SNAP," January 6, 2012 (http://www.fns.usda.gov/snap/rules/Legislation/about.htm).

[167] US Department of Agriculture, "Supplemental Nutrition Assistance Program Participation and Costs," January 6, 2012 (http://www.fns.usda.gov/pd/SNAPsummary.htm).

[168] Getting SNAP, "What is SNAP?" January 6, 2012 (http://www.gettingsnap.org/whatissnap.html).

[169] US Department of Agriculture, "Supplemental Nutrition Assistance Program," January 6, 2012 (http://www.fns.usda.gov/snap/applicant_recipients/eligibility.htm#Resources).

[170] Ibid.

[171] Center for Budget and Policy Priorities, "What is TANF?" January 6, 2012 (http://www.cbpp.org/cms/index.cfm?fa=view&id=936).

[172] US Department of Health and Human Services, "TANF: Total Number of Recipients," January 6, 2012 (http://www.acf.hhs.gov/programs/ofa/data-reports/caseload/2010/2010_recipient_tan.htm).

[173] US Department of Health and Human Services, "About TANF," January 6, 2012 (http://www.acf.hhs.gov/programs/ofa/tanf/about.html).

[174] Ibid.

[175] Social Security Administration, "Unemployment Insurance," January 6, 2012 (http://www.socialsecurity.gov/policy/docs/progdesc/sspus/unemploy.pdf).

[176] US Department of Labor, "News Release," January 12, 2012. January 13, 2012 (http://ows.doleta.gov/press/2012/011212.asp).

[177] US Department of Labor "State Unemployment Insurance," January 6, 2012 (http://workforcesecurity.doleta.gov/unemploy/uifactsheet.asp).

[178] Ibid.

[179] US Department of the Treasury, "Bonds and Securities," January 9, 2012 (http://www.treasury.gov/services/Pages/bonds-securites.aspx).

[180] Office of Management and Budget, Historical Table 1.1—Summary of Receipts, Outlays, Surpluses and Deficits: 1789–2017, February 13, 2012.

[181] Office of Management and Budget, Historical Table 1.2—Summary of Receipts, Outlays, and Surpluses or Deficits as Percentages of GDP: 1930-2017, February 13, 2012.

[182] Recovery Board, "The Recovery Act," December 5, 2011 (http://www.recovery.gov/About/Pages/The_Act.aspx).

[183] Measuring Worth, "What Was the US GDP Then?" November 22, 2011 (http://www.measuringworth.org/usgdp/).

[184] Office of Management and Budget, Historical Table 7.1—Federal Debt at the End of the Year: 1940–2017, February 13, 2012.

[185] US Department of Treasury, "Our History," November 22, 2011. January 10, 2012 (http://www.publicdebt.treas.gov/history/history.htm).

[186] Ibid.

[187] US Government Accountability Office, "Federal Debt: Answers to Frequently Asked Questions, An Update," January 9, 2012 (http://www.gao.gov/new.items/d04485sp.pdf).

[188] US Government Accountability Office, "Federal Debt Basics," January 9, 2012 (http://www.gao.gov/special.pubs/longterm/debt/debtbasics.html).

[189] US Government Accounting Office, "Ownership of Federal Debt," November 22, 2011. (http://www.gao.gov/special.pubs/longterm/debt/ownership.html).

[190] Social Security Administration, "Trust Fund Data," January 9, 2012 (http://www.ssa.gov/oact/ProgData/fundFAQ.html).

[191] US Government Accounting Office, "Federal Debt Basics," November 22, 2011.

[192] Treasury Direct, "Interest Expense on the Debt Outstanding," January 9, 2012 (http://www.treasurydirect.gov/govt/reports/ir/ir_expense.htm).

[193] Office of Management and Budget, Historical Table 7.3—Statutory Limits on Federal Debt: 1940–Current, February 13, 2012.

[194] US Department of the Treasury, "Debt Limit," January 9, 2012 (http://www.treasury.gov/initiatives/pages/debtlimit.aspx).

[195] Congressional Research Service, "Statutory Budget Controls in Effect Between 1985 and 2002," Report R41901, July 1, 2011.

[196] Ibid.

[197] Ibid.

[198] Ibid.

[199] Speaker of the House John Boehner, "Summary of the Revised Budget Control Act of 2011," January 9, 2012 (http://www.speaker.gov/News/DocumentSingle.aspx?DocumentID=254628).

[200] Allison Kopicki, "Most Expect to Give More Than They Receive, Poll Finds," February 11, 2012. February 17, 2012 (http://www.nytimes.com/2012/02/12/us/most-expect-to-give-more-than-they-receive-poll-finds.html).

[201] Reuters Money, "Should Rich People Pay More for Medicare?" September 22, 2011. February 19, 2012 (http://blogs.reuters.com/reuters-money/2011/09/22/should-rich-people-pay-more-for-medicare/).

[202] Office of Management and Budget, "Analytical Perspectives, Budget of the United States Government, Fiscal Year 2013," February 13, 2013

[203] Office of Management and Budget, "Analytical Perspectives, Budget of the United States Government, Fiscal Year 2013", Table 2–3, February 13, 2012.

[204] Office of Management and Budget, Historical Table 1.1—Summary of Receipts, Outlays, and Surpluses or Deficits: 1789–2017, February 13, 2012.

[205] Office of Management and Budget, Historical Table 1.2—Summary of Receipts, Outlays, and Surpluses or Deficits as Percentages of GDP: 1930–2017. February 13, 2012.

[206] Kaiser Family Foundation "U.S. Healthcare Costs." December 1, 2011 (http://www.kaiseredu.org/Issue-Modules/US-Health-Care-Costs/Background-Brief.aspx).

[207] Congressional Budget Office, "Technological Change and the Growth of Healthcare Spending." December 1, 2011 (http://www.cbo.gov/ftpdocs/89xx/doc8947/MainText.3.1.shtml).

[208] Kaiser Family Foundation, "Healthcare Spending in the United States and Selected OECD Countries," April 2011. February 10, 2012 (http://www.kff.org/insurance/snapshot/OECD042111.cfm).

[209] US Department of Health and Human Services, "Affordable Care Act Initiative to Lower Costs, Help Doctors and Hospitals Coordinate Care," August 23, 2011. February 7, 2012 (http://www.hhs.gov/news/press/2011pres/08/20110823a.html).

[210] US Census Bureau, 2010 American Community Survey 3-Year Estimates, Table B18135: "Age By Disability Status By Health Insurance Coverage."

[211] US Department of Health and Human Services, Centers for Medicare and Medicaid, 2010 Actuarial Report on the Financial Outlook for Medicaid, Table 2: "2009 Estimated Enrollment, Expenditures, and Estimated per Enrollee Expenditures, By Enrollment Group," 13. (https://www.cms.gov/ActuarialStudies/downloads/MedicaidReport2010.pdf).

[212] Pew Research Center, "Public Priorities: Deficit Rising, Terrorism Slipping," 23 Jan. 2012. 13 March 2012. (http://www.people-press.org/2012/01/23/section-2-iran-afghanistan-military-policy-u-s-global-image/).

[213] Department of Defense, "Summary of the DoD Fiscal 2013 Budget Proposal," February 13, 2012 (http://www.defense.gov/news/2013budget.pdf).

[214] Department of Defense, "Remarks by Secretary of Defense Robert M. Gates," May 8, 2010 (http://www.defense.gov/speeches/speech.aspx?speechid=1467).

[215] Pew Research Center, "Rethinking Budget Cutting: Fewer Want Spending to Grow, But Most Cuts Remain Unpopular," February 10, 2011. February 27, 2012 (http://pewresearch.org/pubs/1889/poll-federal-spending-programs-budget-cuts-raise-taxes-state-budgets).

[216] US Department of Education, "2013 Budget Continues Investments to Strengthen Workforce and Rebuild American Economy," February

13, 2012. February 13, 2012 (http://www.ed.gov/news/press-releases/us-department-education-2013-budget-continues-investments-strengthen-workforce-a).

[217] Ibid.

[218] US Department of Education, "Fiscal Year 2013 Budget, Summary and Background Information," February 2012, 47. February 27, 2012 (http://www2.ed.gov/about/overview/budget/budget13/summary/13summary.pdf).

[219] Judith L. Pace, "Why We Need to Save (and Strengthen) Social Studies," *Education Week*, December 18 2007. February 27, 2012 (http://www.edweek.org/ew/articles/2007/12/19/16pace.h27.html).

[220] Common Core State Standards Initiative, "The Standards," January 16, 2012. February 27, 2013 (http://www.corestandards.org/the-standards).

Acknowledgments

NPP would like to thank the following for their support:
Monte Belmonte
Madeline Caulfield
Isabelle D'Arcy
Ruth Flower
Kelsey Flynn
Sut Jhally
Ariane Khalfa
Mia Logg
Jeff Napolitano
Ethan Pollack
Hilary Price
Bill Scher
Alwin Schmidt
Laras Sekarasih
Debbie Weinstein
And the social studies department of Chicopee High School.

Guest Contributor
Tom Pappalardo, cover artist and cartoonist
Tom Pappalardo is a professional graphic designer, illustrator, and animator, who works freelance under the name Standard Design. He is best known for his poster designs and flat, clean design work. Tom publishes a weekly comic, *The Optimist*, and is currently working on *Broken Lines*, a graphic novel. He also plays in a guitar and drum duo, The Demographic. He lives in Northampton, Massachusetts.